10 WAYS OF THINKING

BUSINESS LIFE

TAKE CONTROL OF YOUR LIFE

...while you drink a coffee

TEST NEW IDEAS, TRANSFORM YOUR HABITS AND AWAKEN DECISION-MAKING POWER

TEX JERHAND

ISBN: [9781914360039]

@ Cover picture: [Tex Jerhand]

First edition [mar 2021]

"Changing doesn't always mean improving,

but to improve you have to change."

- SIR WINSTON CHURCHILL

Contents

Simple strategy before you start reading the book

If you want a real experience of change in your life and enjoy all the benefits that this book could offer you, you must be aware of reading it with the **RIGHT ATTITUDE.**

1. Decide to change before you start reading

The attitude you have when you start reading is fundamental, make a promise to yourself: **THE COMMITMENT TO TAKE CONTROL OF YOUR LIFE.**

Before reading the first page, take a sheet of paper and write down the 3 **THINGS YOU WILL CHANGE IN YOUR LIFE** when you are done reading the book.

You are probably wondering: how do I know what will change in my life if I have not read the book yet?

And how did you manage to spend money on a book you haven't read yet?

The truth is simple, only that it is within you: **YOU ALREADY KNOW WHAT IS WRONG WITH YOUR LIFE, WHAT OR HOW YOU WOULD LIKE TO IMPROVE.**

The book, for you, must only be an instrument.

Think of the 3 things you would like to improve in your life by reading the book.

Write them immediately and reread them while reading the book at the end of each chapter.

2. Take notes

Changing one's life is a serious matter.

Underline the **key phrases** and if the book really deserves for you, also make some **conceptual maps**.

Commitment helps you develop your true **desire for change**, and thinking about key concepts helps **you memorize them**.

Reaching your change goals will be easier the more effort you put into these phases. And remember that each chapter will help you reflect on something in a more or less interesting way for you, but **only a few points will be really valuable to take control of your life**, or for the goals you wrote yourself before reading the book, these are the notes you will want to write and take the time to meditate on how to apply them.

3. Don't read personal growth books

If you really want to change your life there is no use in continuing to read personal growth books one after the other.

Reading books only serves to fill your mind with notions and continually shifts your focus, too much wood on the embers makes a lot of smoke, but not fire.

So find and read another book only after you have truly transformed your life, changed habits or acquired a new notion of life.

NOW, BEFORE YOU CONTINUE READING, GET ORGANIZED AND APPLY THE STRATEGY RIGHT AWAY: I'M SURE YOU'LL THANK YOU FOR DOING IT!

- Tex Jerhand

INTRODUCTION

The human brain is the most amazing and complex computer machine that people have. He is the one responsible for everything that happens to your body. However, regardless of what a person thinks or how much you use your body, most people use less than 10% of their brain capacity.

In business, it is essential to come up with new business ideas to remain competitive in the business world. As a manager or business owner, you want your collaborators to think from time to time about new business ideas to keep up with the competition.

If you need a fresh idea to advertise your company online, launch a new TV advertisement campaign, build a sales plan, raise profits or just be a better individual, the need to be innovative is at the forefront. It is maybe more important than ever in today's world. Sometimes it seems difficult. Maybe it's because we have many more options today than a decade or two ago. Of course, we are mainly talking about business ideas and financial success. But no matter what happens, it is necessary to find new ideas.

Have you ever read a think tank or attended a motivational seminar or marketing meeting, are you looking forward to getting back to work with tons of new ideas that, you know, have a huge impact on the future growth of your business?

Remember that you are pure potential, you are full of infinite possibilities, and consequently, if you want it, there is nothing that can prevent you from taking control of your life, testing new ideas, transforming your habits and having great decision-making power.

At any time you can become a better person, maintaining the right characteristics and changing the wrong ways of thinking, behaviors, habits, ways of being and posing.

The problem is that a few months later, none of those ideas that you knew you would make more money and grow your business has been implemented or even assessed by your staff as a failure. and quickly forgotten.

Is it the idea that you failed or failed as the owner and manager of your company?

For years you may have tried to position your company for success, or simply take control of your life where you are respected, valued and cared for. However, you can miss your goal,

Your future is determined by the habits that you create today. Your habits are your daily actions. You have to change your habit and change your way of thinking, you think that regulates your action {Turn your Habits}, this is how you achieve your results. You feed on positive thoughts, you change your habits and you get good results.

Changing your habits can be difficult. I was late all the time. I noticed that I was still about 10 minutes behind where I wanted to be.

So I decided it would be easy to prepare to leave 15 minutes earlier. But I noticed that I was so used to being late, rushed to leave on time, that I unconsciously thought I had extra time. The result was that it took me another 15 minutes to prepare to leave!

But I also realized that if I want to find the success I'm looking for, being on time was an important way to change and develop my habit. Time is precious for successful people. If I wanted to integrate with the mentors, colleagues, potential business partners that I had chosen - if I wanted to succeed like them - I had to take the habit of being on time.

During the day we make thousands of decisions every minute. Most of these decisions are made without conscious reflection; instinctively or through responses learned as habits based on a lifelong experience.

Unfortunately, these usual decision-making patterns are preserved in the business world, so that owners react without thinking about changing situations without really thinking. Such behaviour is not appropriate in the business environment where the change is constant. In the current environment, every trait causes disturbing news to be mini-panic, while all the good news is often delivered or ignored. Conversely, in a thriving economy, any encouraging news leads to a frenzy of optimistic responses, while negative situations are considered abnormal and meaningless without decision-making power.

The reality is that none of these scenarios is the result of logical analysis, they are just emotional responses based on the moment.

This is why entrepreneurs need to focus their attention on their instincts, habits, and emotions, realizing that automatic responses in a chaotic business environment are full of dangers.

Many entrepreneurs have always trusted their intuition to make decisions; often with great success that reinforces their belief in themselves and their comfort with the idea that this behaviour will always be successful. In some cases, intuitive decision-makers are truly gifted with extraordinary wisdom and confidence is guaranteed. However, this is rarely the true nature of things. Most of the time, past success comes from luck, from playing in familiar territory, or simply from a problem that, in a booming economy, the tide is lifting all boats.

Until decision-making power is taken - to take over an idea, to buy something, to accept the terms of negotiation, to choose one over the other or to act in any way - there can be no transaction completed. With the most accurate data, the most effective solution or the best idea or moral justice, until there is agreement or action, nothing new happens and there is no change. We can be honest, intelligent, efficient and moral - and buy-in can escape us regardless of "good" or "rational" or the need for new decision-making power.

You can awaken in yourself the decision-making power, that power that will give you the ability not to be dominated by the choices of others but will give you the awareness that not only will you be able to choose personally thanks to the help of trusted people, but that to every personal decision taken, you will have discovered and better known yourself.

After all, every decision-making authority is a problem of change management. Whether it is a personal decision or the result of business, scientific or professional judgments, making a decision is a sum or deduction of something in the status quo that would be influenced by new or different information. So, making a decision is not only about the facts, the inputs/outputs, the risks, the uncertainty or the information obtained, but also about the process of acceptance, acceptance, and flexibility of the scheme.

The secret of success in business is based on what you think of yourself, on how you consider life, a precious asset to be directed towards balance and happiness, certainly not towards excesses and the frantic research for money.

Real business leads you to be happy for having decided to take control of your life, not for being dominated by it and spending your days enslaved by it. The real change lies in yourself because once you improve yourself then everything around you, including your business, will grow accordingly.

I realize that a large part of the decision domain focuses on 'good data', 'rational decisions' or 'reduction of bias', but the subjective systemic part of decision-making power is generally omitted: until Whether there is an acceptable path that is acceptable for the status quo - no matter how effective the results are - the decision-making power is incomplete

You will learn that courage will serve you to make the right decisions and make the necessary changes, using fear as a means of achieving your ultimate goal, not as an insurmountable obstacle.

You can get out of the cliche that society, family or friends have given you throughout your life and finally be yourself, overcoming the limits that your mind has set itself, and realizing that you can be or do much more than you mistakenly believe.

It will be a fundamental step to take control of your life, aware that to do it you must act immediately without delaying and thus win indecision because knowing how to decide at the right time determines the success or failure of any business you are doing or are in about to start.

Chapter 1

PERSONAL RESPONSIBILITYAND TAKING IT RIGHTLY

It is only when we take full responsibility for the actions that depend on our choices or our behaviours that we lay solid foundations for truly changing the various situations in our lives. Blaming the circumstances and the surrounding environment for achieving negative results, for the inability to act or for the feelings that you cannot manage, only leads to not focusing the true key to unlocking the potential for change. Taking responsibility for both positive and negative results will allow you not only to understand that it is up to you to want to change, but that you also have the power to do so and to take control of your life. This will help to be able to distinguish and quickly adopt different ways to create or improve your business.

Ways to take personal responsibility

"You have to take personal responsibility. It is something you are responsible for because of the decision-making power.

I believe it is possible to create better results for ourselves by making better decisions. I am not saying that bad things will never happen, but we are responsible for the choices we make every day in our lives. I have worked with clients who blame the economy, blame their husbands and blame their competitors for not doing more business and earning more money. Or the entrepreneur, who complains about working all the time and has no personal time. These are all choices that we make free and we must take personal responsibility for the results and decisions that we make.

1. Recognize that you are solely responsible for the choices of your life:

   The work in which you live, where you live, your partner or partner, the house in which you live, the car in which you drive, the friends you maintain.

   These are things that we have chosen, and if you are not satisfied with some (or all) of these things, it's time to test a new idea or a different choice. Small incremental changes can produce very large results!

2. Accept that you are responsible for every promotion and non-promotion:

   You create your life with every action and inactivity that you undertake. So often I listen to one of my clients who tells how they "could have done this" or "could have benefited". It's true. Several opportunities come to mind every day and test business ideas, but we do not see them as an opportunity. We consider it "too much work", "too difficult to do", "not what I wanted" and we do not take action.

3. Accept that you cannot blame others for your choices:

At one time or another, we have all blamed our brothers and sisters, parents, spouse or partner or friend for some injustice in our lives, but you cannot blame others for your new ideas and choices. No one else is responsible. If you want things to be different in your life, it's your responsibility to make the change!

4. Have positive expectations, even in the case of adversity:

   It is easier said than done, I know. But it is possible to have positive expectations and to take positive action somehow every day, to change the things that you are not satisfied or dissatisfied with your work or your life. A person with a negative or cynical attitude will never achieve much. This is because when an opportunity presents itself, the negative mind will find a reason (or 100 reasons) not to act upon it.

5. Accept to choose the outcome of life:

   By taking personal responsibility, we begin to move from our current situation to a better life. We have total control over all the decisions we make, and our choices.

Personal responsibility

How often do you hear yourself say things like "I can't", "If only", "I have to", "There is nothing I can do", "I wish", "She 'irritates'," has no one told me, "it started"?

How often do you let your situation control your reactions instead of using your actions to control your situation? If you respond to everything that happens to you with a feeling of helplessness, then it is no wonder that you feel helpless. When you look outside of yourself for the answers to your problems, you come across a world outside of your control and soon your life starts to lose control because whatever techniques you try, you will not be able to change anything in substance.

Take relationships, for example. Most relationships are, to a certain extent, a form of addiction. If you have to communicate with people who have a bad day, then their bad day will reflect your day. Whether you have a good day or not depends on whether everyone around you has a good day. Addiction is a scary place because you have no control over the people or situations you depend on.

For many people, when someone around them has a bad day, their immediate response is to try to control the situation. They try to control the person by talking about 'sense' with them, or they try to solve the person's problems - an equally pointless choice in their research of ideas.

When you try to solve the problems of others, you ultimately create their problems, your problems. In the end, people start to expect you to intervene and solve all their problems. Don't have enough problems? Moreover, people have to deal with their problems, otherwise, they will never learn what to do when their problems come back. The river likes to send us the same problems until we are sure that we have solved things ourselves. When we try to solve problems for other people, we waste all our energy trying to solve things that we cannot fix. We can solve the problem, but the situation remains the same. And if we fail to resolve the situation, the problem reappears; until we finally became exhausted, bitter, frustrated and cynical.

Many of us strive to improve our situations by trying to control things beyond our control. We are finally getting frustrated. Or worse, we just use what life has given us as an excuse for doing nothing to change our situation. We believe that the world is in control of everything while we are helpless and impeccable. Our birth, our education, and our environment have all determined our lives; and, poor people, nothing that we can do will change these things.

If you think so, you are not alone. Our entire society is strongly written in this kind of mentality. But be careful when buying this type of script. The scripts you play in your head become true to you. Consider the power of decision-making power. The more you think your life is getting out of hand, the more your life has got out of hand.

Chapter 2

EMOTIONAL MANAGEMENT

Emotions are part of what makes us human. They mark our lives by giving us unforgettable moments and moments. There is a wide range of feelings, and they all contribute to forming our character and our being in the world about ourselves and our neighbour. Unfortunately, the wrong management of our emotional character can condition us to the point of ruining or even damaging the growth path, closely linked to our business. Knowing how to manage one's emotional state is the requirement for those who know how to manage themselves and who masterfully manage to get out of emotional states that leave them firm and unproductive. It does not mean transforming your habits in a radical way or stopping trying certain emotions, but knowing how to manage them, resize them if necessary or develop them, for personal and collective good. To take control of your life you need to acquire strong decision-making power over your emotions.

The importance of emotional management

One of the most difficult things to learn when it comes to working with the law of attraction is how we can control our emotions. It is such an important skill if you want to attract the things you want in your life that you have to put time and energy into it. We attract what we think and feel the most, so the more we let our negative emotions dominate, the more negative things we will attract. Sometimes it can be difficult to stay positive when the world around us launches what it does, regardless of which world we need to manage our emotional state.

Every day we all have to deal with people or situations or things in our lives that make us feel depressed or angry or some negative emotions. It is a normal part of life. The difference is how you allow it to affect you. Several things can happen from a failed relationship to failed friendships, problems and stress at work. Your ability to monitor your goals and manage your emotions and keep them positive is directly in line with your success and your ability to attract whatever you want in your life.

There are certain things you can do to keep your emotions in a positive state. First of all, you have to remember where you are going, no matter what is happening right now. This is just a temporary situation right now, but your goals and the future you want to build are part of your daily life. A runner does not focus on the pain in his legs or the people next to him. He keeps an eye on the finish line and pushes with everything he has until he crosses that line. Then he can look back on the pain and the other runners and what happened because it all belonged to the past then, and as we all know, the past has faded away.

Another important thing to remember when things happen is that this one thing is not your entire life. If you have someone at work who is causing you problems, remember that this person is only that person. They are not your partner, nor your hobbies, nor all the other things that you have in your life. Goodwill always surpasses badly if you think about it. There is always something better in your life and more positive if you take the time to see it. We often allow what's happening right now to cloud our entire emotional state and our lives. We allow things to consume our thinking, and that will only slow down your progress and performance.

Don't forget to control your emotions, otherwise, your emotions will control you. Keep an eye on the goal and stay there no matter what happens. Even if things get so bad that it seems like nothing, but bullets and bombs are flying at you, keep moving. Keep an eye on the price. Even with death a step behind you, keep moving. Manage your emotions and keep them positive, and as soon as you begin to recognize that they are evolving towards the negative, change your head and your heart. The universe rewards those who act and manage their lives.

Emotional management - A must in business

Managing emotions is a daunting task for some, but an essential skill for success in business and personal relationships. We all have and experience and experience new emotions, whether we like it or not. Emotion management is mainly about unpleasant emotions: anger, fear, frustration, depression, hopelessness. Emotions are the feelings we experience today, such as happiness, pride, boredom, sadness, anger, and frustration. Emotions are part of our daily lives as they move through the body and affect our state of mind, our performance, our health, and our energy. Emotions cannot be helped. The emotions that we do not even realize that we feel can affect our thoughts and behaviour; they can also travel from person to person like a virus. Because of this viral condition, it is of the utmost importance for those who cannot only influence their own emotions but also understand the need to control mood and perhaps influence others with their decision-making power.

The management is in a unique position to dictate the pulse and the rhythm at his workplace. Without this component of emotional management, a working environment can become toxic.

Those in leadership positions are often not good at working with people and therefore spend a lot of their time avoiding and/or developing strategies for treating, avoiding or getting rid of people in difficulty. Much leadership is actually about dealing with emotions. Emotions are also essential for inspiring leadership. These managers often lack the decision-making power, necessary human skills, communication skills, and leadership skills to influence the emotional tone of the workplace. This is critical supervision by senior managers who do not receive or provide the training necessary to create a positive emotional tone. In turn, the state of mind, ideas, emotions, and general dispositions of colleagues affect work performance, decision-making power, creativity, revenue, teamwork, negotiations, and leadership.

For management to be able to fully control the emotions of the workplace, it must have control over itself, that of itself and that of its colleagues. Colleagues must be positive at work - but this must be supported by senior management. Colleagues need positive feedback and if they don't see it coming, or are not even recognized for their work, they will look elsewhere. This ensures revenue and higher costs and lower performance. Many colleagues in today's economy do not hesitate to go further than anyone else instead of touching this aspect. They do not take into account the long-term costs of losing an employee during downtime and retraining a new colleague.

One of the most basic things needed to improve colleague attitudes and create a "culture of love" is to adopt systems that recognize and reward these positive attitudes and behaviors. When managers are manipulative and treat colleagues as "equipment" rather than human beings, bad attitudes follow. And a workplace where emotions are rampant can discourage colleagues, sellers, and customers. Similarly, the manager must ensure that he manages the negative emotional attitudes of his team so that these attitudes are not reflected in their performance. Managers must also learn to set a good example by defining how they can treat their pain in a positive way, which can inspire others to manage their difficult situations differently. An example of a manager being dragged down at the start of every day as he walked past the desk of a colleague who growled or did not acknowledge. The manager took control and simply started following another route through the office. If the company loses money and is affected by contraction, the manager, who feels stressed and overwhelmed, must transfer his despair to his colleague. Or should the manager look cheerful and pretend that nothing has happened? the manager can convey both authentic and positive emotions and say something like: "I know you're worried. The ability to create decision-making power and to test new ideas to generate positive emotions in times of successful management stress.

The main implication is that organizations should focus on hiring managers with high emotional and social skills and also provide EI training and development opportunities for managers to enable them to create a positive organizational environment. Effective listening is also an important aspect of learning.

Also, listening to testing new ideas is an important skill and must be learned. Feedback must take into account the needs of both the donor and the recipient. Otherwise, it can be destructive if the needs and feelings of all involved are not taken into account. Listen to words, body language and emotions to understand the conscious and unconscious needs of the player. By feeling heard, many negative consequences of an unfortunate or upset employee can be reduced if they are not completely stopped.

Controlling emotions does not mean that you deny or ignore them. Never tell a colleague that he should not feel this. Feelings are a biological reaction, a circumstance, an event or a stressor and cannot be helped. The way you can help is to recognize feelings and to help the colleague consider potential positive choices to resolve his current feelings. Take a minute to think about the importance of turning your habits into new ideas and how you can be a good active listener in terms of body language. Decision-making power is an effective tool to reduce the emotionality of a situation. Any manager or team leader who can acquire these skills will discover that his team will improve the overall loyalty and performance of the company. Controlling emotions is something that needs to be addressed, not avoided to be successful.

Steps to improve your emotional management skills

Good emotion management is a skill. You must learn and practice it before you can perfect it. If you want to commit to "skill" learning now, here are the five steps you should start with:

- Identify your approach to your emotions: try to be aware and understand how you react to certain environmental stimuli. Some questions you can ask yourself are:
    - How to deal with problems and failures?

- o How easily do I get over my problems?

- How does the way I socialize not only affect my emotions but above all in my business life
- Develop your emotional awareness. It is sort of the result of the self-examination that you do in step number one. By becoming aware of how you react to things, you begin to realize which specific effects of your emotions you have to work with.
- Choose and use your most important emotional tools. These tools are the intrinsic factors that help you meet challenges. This can include your self-confidence and your ability to forgive easily. The idea is to identify your strengths and use them to improve yourself. For example, if you are the type that easily forgets mistakes, use them to forgive yourself when you make mistakes and come to life as quickly as possible.
- Release your emotional trauma. If you have something to do with something or someone, stand up for it and finish it once and for all.
- Learn to communicate effectively how you feel and to test new ideas. Learning to share your thoughts with others helps you in two ways. First, it helps you to let go of all your pent-up emotions inside, and second, it helps you to develop a support group that you can rely on if you need advice or guidance.
- These are the five steps you must take to try to effectively manage your depression. The learning process can be difficult and initially difficult, but once you have the skills, you are ready to go.

Emotional management - How to see it in a positive light

I often read or hear statements that look like this:

I struggle with this mantra because it can distract us from valid (often uncomfortable) feelings that contain important information for us. I can testify to the important role that avoiding emotions has played in my life. Years of therapy have shown that my unrecognized anger toward my family has greatly contributed to my obsession with health and illness. If you mentioned an illness, I thought I had it! Although I realize that this is an extreme example, it certainly illustrates the power emotions have over us if we avoid them. Our instinct is to assume that the "feeling" of our feelings will immobilize us.

The reverse is true.

Giving time to our emotions is liberating, and often provides us with information about ourselves that we previously had no access to. When we ignore feelings, they don't disappear. Instead, they get angry and express themselves in other, less healthy ways.

"The power of vulnerability" explains how we are a society that numbs our feelings by drinking, smoking and eating too much. We not only anaesthetize ourselves in a self-destructive way such as addiction but also by other behaviors. We strive for perfection or opt for the "easier" act of pointing fingers and blaming others for everything wrong in our world. Interestingly, the definition of guilt is "a means to relieve pain and discomfort."

Looks familiar?

The key to lighting and solution:

- See the feelings you feel
- Recognize your feelings
- Accept your feelings

This creates 2 opportunities:

- We receive important information about what we can do about a certain situation or circumstance.
- "Making an emotion happen" is very soothing.

Here are 5 useful steps to deal with your emotions:

Am I upset? Am I feeling angry? Am I feeling left out? or Am I feeling hurt?

Most of the time when I ask myself questions of how I feel, the problem doesn't even seem as intense as I thought it was. Second, always remember that your emotions are there for a goal and purpose. Acknowledge your emotions even though you don't understand them at the moment. Never make your emotion wrong. That will not make any problem less intense. Instead appreciate the emotions.

This may sound crazy but it works! Third, get curious about that emotion. It will interrupt your pattern, and why this emotion showed up? Fourth, be confident about the emotion, just remember when the last time you had the same feeling and how you got through it. Every emotion we faced we got through it and know how to deal with it. Five, get excited about that emotion and take action right away.

Try this method, I always like to play pictures in my head or a video for the next time this happens. The next time you feel angry, play that you're in your house, (blue, green, or a trailer if you're that type of person) and all of a sudden you hear a loud knock! when you open the door you see Mr angry screaming at you making no sense. What I would do is change the little carpet by the front door that says "Welcome" to " Not Welcome" and slam the door while you clap your hands. This works for every emotion and keeps repeating this exercise

- Note the emotion (maybe the one you have now) without judging it.
- Name the emotion.
- Be "with" the emotion. Let the feeling happen and accept your humanity.
- Pay attention to the message that it might have for you. What can it teach you?

Recognize yourself to better understand your feelings. It may take a while to get the hang of it, but you will succeed, and it's worth it!

Chapter 3

THE SUM OF YOUR DECISION

Who can decide the course of our life? There are infinite answers, just as infinite are the variables for each of them; but they all fall into two main categories: "we" and "them". By "them" we mean everything that is beyond our every possible intervention, such as certain decisions of others or what is related to the external environment. For these decisions we cannot do anything, we have no decision-making power, and therefore we can often follow them by grasping the positive side, thus leaving out what limits our work. Instead, we can focus on "we". It is in this category that all of our margin of action resides, and that is why knowing how to make decisions is fundamental to developing ourselves and our business. We will not always have the opportunity to reflect a lot and we will have little time to make the best possible decision. Here comes the experience, the preparation, but also our trained and conscious predisposition to know how to make wise and safe decisions by gathering the necessary information and reaching the correct conclusions with reasoning. It is thanks to the sum of the right decisions that you can truly take control of your life and thus improve your business.

Decisions or lack of decision making are very important for your life situation. You are where your decisions made you. Have you decided to take this job or make this investment by choosing to live where you are or to go to this university or college instead of the other? The decisions you made have affected your position in life, the amount of money you earn, the partner you work with, and everything you have now.

We cannot go back and change the decisions we have made in our lives so far. We can make various powerful decisions now and in the future. If you do not like the place where you currently live, you can decide to change your decision-making power. You can try to make various decisions based on knowledge. You can start research and research to make different decisions to change your life. You can start today.

What would you change now? Do you regret? Are there unfulfilled areas in your life? Start knowing yourself today and understand why you do what you do. Do personality tests to help you understand yourself. Consider making decisions and testing new ideas, study your personalities without decision-making authority, and see strengths and weaknesses. You can see why you act and act in a certain way.

How to improve your decision making

How do you proceed if you are confronted with a decision-making situation? Do you decide right away and do you postpone your decision to a certain point or test new ideas?

Although many experts recommend that quick decision-making has many advantages, it can also lead to errors. And many decisions are irreversible, if not lead to unpleasant results. A systematic method must be applied to get the most out of your decision-making power.

Of course, good decisions are the result of a good understanding of the decision-making situation. If you are confused or have a lot of uncertainty in mind, numbers can help you improve the outcome of your decision.

How does this technique work? The method is simple. Follow the steps below.

How to improve decision-making skills:

Step 1. Always make a list of the two sides of your decision

Find a sheet of paper, create a layout with two columns and write "Advantages" in the left column and the right column, "Disadvantages". Make a list of all the advantages and disadvantages that you can think of in connection with your decision.

Step 2. Evaluate your list of advantages and disadvantages

Assess any advantage or disadvantage that you mention using a 10-point scale ranging from unimportant to very important. If the advantage or disadvantage is not significant, you can simply classify it as "1", but if you think it is a major advantage or disadvantage, you can write it down "10" as much as possible. If it is not unimportant or very important, your speed will be between the extremes.

Step 3. Add all points

Summarize the points you have given for each advantage or disadvantage of your decision. Of the total number of points, you can easily see which column has more points than the others. You can hire the one with the highest number of points.

If the points are more or less similar, you can repeat the steps without referring to the previous one. This is called iteration. You can do this three times to confirm your decision.

Evaluate your decision

After applying the above steps and making a decision where the benefits outweigh the disadvantages, you assess your decision by answering the following questions.

- Is your decision urgent?

  Do you have to make this decision? Otherwise, it is better to give more time to think about your decision. The uncertainty decreases over time. Procrastination can offer more opportunities to solve problems.

- Does your decision change your life?

  Which decisions change lives? The decision to get married or change jobs is an example. This involves a lifelong commitment or the abandonment of an equally important choice, so you need to think carefully about the consequences of your decision.

- Who will be affected by your decision?

  If you are the only person affected by your decision-making power, your decision must be quick. If something goes wrong, no one is to blame except you. If your decision influences others, it is wise to consult them too.

Further tips to improve your decision making

As a professional, whether you own your own business or work for someone else, you always want to have the best possible decision-making power. This means good business decisions, good financial decisions, good product decisions if you sell products from your new Chinese manufacturer, as well as good decisions for employees. An error in one of these areas can have a significant impact on your business results.

No doubt owning or running a business in the current market and that the economy creates stress for even the strongest person. If you feel the effects of stress, you have to slow down, test new ideas and identify the causes of your stress. The first question to be asked is "is this something that I can change so that it is not that stressful for me?" If the answer is yes, it is now time to make these changes. Every reduction in stress is an improvement in your level of functioning, and therefore in decision-making. On the other hand, if stress is something that you cannot influence, you must learn to deal with it. Part of this adjustment could be to avoid certain situations that may or may not be possible. The biggest part of coping is learning to deal with your stress so that it does not cause any problems in decision making power and, more importantly, your health.

With a little stress, you tend to have an energy boost as stress hormones circulate through your body. This can give you a moment of great clarity or creativity, both of which can be of benefit to your business. The most important thing is not to let your stress continue so that it loses its effectiveness and becomes a harmful aspect in your daily life.

If you talk to a procrastinator, he will tell you that he needs the stress of a deadline to work. So they postponed their work to the last possible minute and then seemed to rush like crazy to finish the job on time. They may think that they are working at their peak, but chances are that if they would learn to do the work in an organized way over time, they would do better. They are wrong in this crazy way of procrastinating until the last minute because they think it is an advantage to their way of working.

Although you have now learned that unmanageable stress can affect your business skills and decision-making power, you may not realize the toll that constant stress can have on your health. This is reason enough to do everything possible to reduce your stress. You know you want to stay healthy so that you can stay longer.

The secret to success to improve your decision making

The level of success that you achieve in life and/or in business is directly proportional to the quality and quantity of your decision-making power.

"Doing is not difficult. Deciding to do it."

Because you see that nothing happens until a decision is made. You've probably heard that nothing happens until a sale is made but think about it. When you made a decision, you sold yourself by testing new ideas.

The problem is that people sometimes have difficulty making even the simplest decisions and get stuck.

One of the reasons for this is that people are not only free to choose their path; often they also have a multitude of choices. And while the latter can be a blessing, on the one hand, it can also be a curse, because when faced with too many options, the mind gets confused and its decision-making capacity diminishes.

Unfortunately, indecision can derail your chances of success.

Successful men make decisions by taking power quickly and changing them very slowly if necessary. Men who fail to make decisions that, if any, take power very slowly and change them often and quickly. "

Indecision and procrastination are twin brothers. People postpone making decisions because they don't have to act. However, they shoot themselves in the foot because they cannot move towards their goals if they do not make a decision.

Often the route to your goal is not direct and you have to keep adjusting the direction of your route until you reach your destination. And the more you improve your decision-making power, the fewer mistakes you make.

So how are you going to improve your decision-making power? Well, you start with the next decision that you have to make. "The way you do everything is the way you do everything."

In other words, if you have weak decision-making power, it will not only manifest itself when you have to make an important decision. It appears in all facets of your life. You probably hesitate to decide which shoes you wear, which lunch restaurant or whether you drive or use public transport to go to your meeting.

So make it a habit to make simple decisions quickly. Also, pay attention and praise yourself when you do this. Practice this tirelessly for at least 30 days. You will find that it becomes easier to make more difficult decisions because you have installed a new way to change your habits.

Also note the positive effects of each of your decisions, because you can be sure that, like any decision that you don't make, there are costs involved, every decision you make has an advantage. In other words, make a regular cost-benefit analysis of the most important decisions you make. You see, for the moment you may be undecided, but you may not fully take into account what your decision costs.

For example, how much did you lose when you hesitated to close this deal? How much did you potentially lose if you did not apply for this position, even though it was perfect for you?

However, it is also important to do the opposite and to acknowledge what you have achieved by being decisive. Pay attention to both material and immaterial benefits. When you do this, you will quickly recognize all the benefits of decisiveness and you will find that your determination, as well as the level of success that you achieve in life, will be leaps and bounds.

Decision-making power is an important leadership skill. People do not trust someone undecided. However, you are the most important person to lead successfully in this life.

Your life is the result of all the choices you make, consciously and unconsciously. If you can control your life in the selection process, you can take control of all aspects of your life. You can find the freedom that comes to being in charge to have yourself.

Chapter 4

AWARENESS OF OWN GOALS. THE FIRST THING IN LIFE

A ship without a clear destination to reach will pass the entire crossing at the mercy of the waves. A life without clear objectives to pursue risks being used chaotically, with the danger of not reaching even one of them.

We often hear the advice to "live day to day", but if not contextualized, this advice pushes people not to focus on important aspects of their lives and moves them away from conscious planning of their short, medium and long-term goals. These goals are what motivates us to change, to improve ourselves, to take the necessary steps to achieve our goals and which in part will allow us to see some of our dreams come true. Nobody needs to have millions of possibilities and not to plan any of them, perhaps for fear of making a mistake, and to hide behind the "alive to the day and so I feel free". Each of us needs to find the right goals and build the opportunities to achieve them one after the other. This can only be achieved by arranging in time reasonable goals linked together, to see over time the actual progress that our efforts are producing.

To transform your habits not to let them lead you, test new ideas, make sure that your life is not distorted by the change but that you take control of your life and thus decide the route.

Our values are the compass that, through the choices, we make every day, give the precise direction to our life. For this reason, deciding on the right values in time will allow us not to spend energy on something unproductive or, worse still, wrong. If we give priority to business we will not have the right values that will allow us to make right choices in life and will ruin our relationships and our "I", which is why we must find the right balance between the true priorities of life and remaining aspects. To do this we must reflect and place on our scale of values the things that are the most important, then everything else will come accordingly. Doing the opposite would only lead to not picking up anything that matters. We need to be clear about what matters most to ourselves.

So if you want to take control of your life and have strong decision-making power over your choices, you must be able to choose well.

Be the hero in your Life

Some things happen to us that we blame on chance or circumstance or maybe even fate. If we're down with bad luck and things just aren't going great, we sometimes dismiss it with a smile and a nod and say "better luck next time". We throw a lot of things to chance and just hope for the best. This is not necessarily a good way of thinking. This bad habit of letting go of things that we can control leaves us with little opportunity for growth and improvement. What one must always aim for is to be the hero in your own life.

Take control of your life and never let anything faze you. Once you set your mind on something, never stop until you have accomplished it. Greet every roadblock with a humongous leap. Being the hero in your life entails courage and also a deep understanding of oneself. First, you have to evaluate yourself, see your strengths and weaknesses. Find out the things that you are extremely good at and the things about you that need improvement.

Finding the good things about yourself will allow you to zero in on a reachable goal. Work on the good things about you, polish them, be the best in your chosen field. Be the hero. Express your strengths in every way imaginable. It has always been believed that no matter what you do, so long as you are passionate about it and so long as you are quite good at it, you will be able to profit from it. Profit could translate to anything, but the bottom line is, no matter what you do, the reward is great if you do it excellently.

Making use of your talents in profitable ways allows you to become the hero in your life. You are uplifting yourself to unimaginable heights, making you take the moon as you reach for the stars. There is nothing quite like moving up in whatever ladders you choose to climb on through your sheer willpower and passion to make things work. Self-actualization comes from reaping benefits out of your hard work. You contribute to society with your unique qualities and you hone that and perfect that craft until everything that comes out of your mouth, your brain, and your hands is gold.

Picking yourself up and moving forward is a characteristic of a would-be hero in your life. If you can aim for the stars, work hard and when you fall, stand up on your own, you know that you are in control.

And this rock-solid control and self-awareness will grant you many opportunities for profit and happiness that you can only imagine.

Goal achievement - Why people fail and how you can succeed

For many people, successful goal achievement can be elusive. People are often good at setting goals but a poor rate of success in actually achieving them. And a primary reason for this is that, apart from those who don't take action at all, many people don't finish what they start. They give up on their goals.

That's why we pull hamstrings in the marathon of life. It's because it's much easier for us not to finish than it is for us to fail.

However, it only seems easier in the short-term. In the long-term, the mental anguish that comes with living an unfulfilled life is very hard to bear. And, make no doubt about it, if you are not working on achieving goals that are worthy of you then you will feel unfulfilled.

Apart from the illusion that abandoning your goals is the easy option. There are many other reasons you give up on your goals including:

- You were pursuing the wrong goal.
- You perceive that going after your goal would be too tough.
- You are not confident that you can achieve your goal.

And the chances are that if not achieving your goals has become a habit then the underlying reason will often be the same each time.

However, there's also another reason why people don't achieve their goals. Paradoxically, the best way for you to achieve your goals is to give up. However, it's not the goal itself that you give up on. The key is to give up any attachment to the outcome of what it is you're striving to achieve.

So when you set a goal you have to believe that:

1. The goal is possible to achieve, and

2. You can achieve the goal.

Once you complete this step you will have your goal on the first plane of existence.

Then let's go.

Trust that, if you do your part, the Universe will work with you to help you bring your goal into fruition or the Universe might reward you with something different.

Now whether or not you perceive that thing to be better than what you originally asked for is entirely down to your perception. If you don't succeed in getting what you originally wanted you may think that you have failed. However, the outcome you regard as failure is merely feedback.

Yet, many people go out of their way to avoid 'failure'. And they are successful in doing this but they do so at the expense of their personal growth because success and failure go hand in hand.

The Universe is forever expanding and we are part of the Universe and so it's our nature to expand or to grow. You do this by setting and striving for challenging goals because this is what stretches you and expands your consciousness or awareness. Achieving your goals is only part of the story it's the personal growth you experience during your goal achievement journey that is more important.

And we're designed to continually expand our awareness. So when you lawfully pursue your goals, i.e. by the Universal Laws, the Universe conspires with you to help you achieve them.

This is why, when you're not on purpose and when you're not continually working on improving yourself and pursuing your dreams, you feel conflicted. You may give because you fear to fail but remember that to the Universe there's no such thing as failure. There's only feedback.

There's a web site called Animoto where you can submit your images; select or upload a music track and then it will sync your images with the music automatically.

Here's the thing. You know what the raw ingredients are but you have no idea what the finished product will look like. Sometimes the result is great but other times it doesn't quite work out the way you want it to.

In the latter case, you simply ask Animoto to remix it and you can keep doing this until you get a result you're happy with.

The Universe works similarly.

So there are three key factors to achieving your goals:

1. Let go of any attachment to the outcome,

2. Finish what you set out to do, and

3. Try again if the first time if things don't quite work out the way you want them to.

The certain way to achieve any goal

The powerful strategy to consider:

1. Succeeding in my goal is non-negotiable.

   Surrender is not part of your vocabulary here and no halfway mark says you can give up. Remember what Yoda in Stars Wars said? Those few words uttered from a puppet in a movie left an indelible impression on me and hit the mark. They may have to have set their compasses on a different course to reach a goal, it may have taken longer or they may have needed to change their path at times, but their journey to that goal was non-negotiable, and that is the attitude to adopt.

   There is a great way to ensure that you become responsible for the changes you want to make.

2. I make myself accountable.

   Now here is a challenge that is necessary if you are to achieve your goals, no matter how big or small.

   For example, if you give up smoking and go through the 3-day flames of hell side effects, they may be so influenced by your tantrums, mood swings, anger fits or gross verbalization of how bad you feel, they may sabotage you right there and then encourage you to take up smoking again because your negativity cannot be managed. You must find a person who will not sabotage your efforts, a colleague you admire, or someone who has accomplished what you want to accomplish and is ready to assist you.

As a budding Internet Marketer, I initially had problems with time management as I allowed myself to be distracted by family members, phone calls and Facebook when I began working from home. I enlisted the aid of a buddy, someone I didn't know very well and I kept a timesheet of exactly what I was doing every day for 2 months and sent it off to him each week.

I am aware of being distracted and can stop it from happening now.

3. I have a positive outcome.

   For a good cause, you have chosen to make a change, you have the leverage you need, which is some sort of pain you want to move away from and some pleasurable result you want to move towards. If you are clear about how you have not been served by your old habit, addiction, career, relationship, etc., then make sure you have a target worth striving for, one that is achievable, and that you want to get and hold in your heart because the positive needs to outweigh the negative. Remain calm and steady in your pursuit and remember to make it fun.

Achieving goals: Best practices

- I change because I choose to
- I step towards my goal with calm self-assurance and maintain this attitude throughout
- I plan to win

- Succeeding in my goal is non-negotiable
- I make myself accountable
- I have a positive outcome

Chapter 5

CREATE TRUE GROWTH RELATIONSHIPS

We were not born to live alone. Within us, we feel the desire to socialize and live in close contact with our fellow humans. We create various forms of business by relating to our neighbour and we are business promoters of others. A fundamental aspect to guarantee this economic circle where we are the architects of our business is the ability to create and enhance positive relationships with other people who come into contact with us. Both the employees with whom we work closely, but also the people who come in and out of our daily lives. Those who manage to create bonds and attract people to themselves have much more chances of being followed in their goal and helped to achieve it. Often it is only thanks to the help of more minds or more arms that goals have been achieved that alone could not even have been designed. If we dedicate the right time and attention to the people around us, we will only benefit from it, because we will easily find those bridges that unite us and that will allow us over time to build bonds of trust and mutual respect. A handful of friends who work with us for a single purpose are worth much more than dozens of people who do it only out of a sense of duty. It is only with them that there will be real business growth. To have a good business it is not enough to test new ideas, but also to make them work thanks to a good team and excellent teamwork.

Let's not forget that to achieve real goals, you always need the help of others, so let's not disdain those who sincerely want to help us in the realization of our dream, also because it could be the same, and dreaming in two is much more beautiful and easier than do it yourself.

Having a powerful network is an important part of business success. Technical success comes from the skills of individuals. Although building a network would definitely be simpler if you are inherently part of a world of business and cash, all you need to create a good network is to be willing to meet new people and move out of your comfort zone.

As its popularity implies, networking often doesn't have to be as soul-stealing. Only a series of colleagues, teammates and acquaintances are networks. And relationships are balanced within good networks. People assist each other equally and truly care for each other's well-being and success.

Networking can't be one-sided in that vein. You've got to help them if you want help from others. Connecting you with people who are experts on what you're trying to do is one of the most beneficial things I think people can do.

So I try to think of who I know that might help them if a friend or acquaintance tells me what they're working on. They do the same for me in exchange.

Reach out to individuals in your network daily. Tell them what they are up to and how you can assist them. That strengthens and makes your relationship mutually beneficial.

I know how tempting it can be to hesitate, hedge and hope that what you want is guessed by others. Asking for someone's support may feel awkward.

But you have to ask for it in order to get what you want. For the other party, too, it's easier because they don't have to guess what you need and the link is more available.

Of course, money is the most inconvenient thing to ask for. My company focused on setting up our crowdfunding campaign two years ago. When we began, we veiled our demands in words like, "if you want" and "if you can spare it." We were far more successful when we made our language more straightforward about halfway through our campaign.

Getting out of the office is one of the best ways to expand your network. You just don't know what individuals you need to communicate with. If you did, it would be as easy to communicate with them as firing off a fast note.

But it's the unexpected people who can connect to the network in a lot of situations. To develop good relationships in all facets of your life with individuals.

Strategies for relationship building in order to thrive in business

Unfortunately, people with a high degree of imagination who are great at inventing stuff frequently do not have good interpersonal skills or interests.

I see a high degree of dissatisfaction from individuals in this group as a mentor to aspiring entrepreneurs, who have personally created great solutions but cannot turn them into a company. They don't know that it takes relationships to run a business.

I firmly believe that, just like any other skill, the talent to create relationships effectively can be mastered, even if you are an introvert like me. Much like learning other abilities that you need to accomplish the goals you have set, it takes effort and concentration.

You need to establish relationships with a wide variety of individuals in industry, including customers, colleagues, workers, and, of course, clients.

The following approaches to stepping up our relationship are up a notch:

1. By diversifying the networks, create fresh relationships. In your immediate circle, push yourself to go beyond individuals, and those you know well, to touch and nurture a real partnership with at least one supplier, a client, and a competitor. The next step is to find specific entities, such as the media and government, from unrelated organizations.

2. Give as much from each relationship as you intend to get. Successful business partnerships need reciprocity-not a half-hearted, one-way effort. Offer and provide assistance, link individuals, or exchange knowledge from the industry or non-profit sector.

Only then can you feel fulfilled and, when you need support, find others willing to respond.

3. Spend quality time on main relationships selectively. Spend time with your most valuable clients, your most efficient workers, and leaders who can make the most of your organization's effects. In the near future and the long term, these partnerships will produce returns. Stop the pit of idle and ego-building conversations.

4. Keep your attention on the social and business landscape that is local. Pay attention to the links, loyalties, and networks that form your culture. Recognize the expectations, principles and preferences that form the behaviour of the individuals you need.

This will help you build a long-lasting and productive network for your business interests that you can optimize.

5. To solve key social problems, apply your time, brand, and money. Develop a set of relationships with individuals with common values, interests, and goals. Working with them to address common social issues will turn them into your company's dedicated supporters and make them your most effective allies in developing other relationships.

6. Prune, refresh, and periodically reshape the networks. Nurture relationships between people that are important to your company

carefully and frequently. Drive contacts into your inactive network whose utility has diminished over time.

Identify new partnerships that are essential to your company's future on a regular basis, and identify strategies to develop these ties.

In all relationship building efforts, I do give some points of caution:

More connections are not necessarily better. There aren't necessarily wider networks for highly successful business leaders. Be cautious about the relationships you make, listen carefully to circumstances where value can be added and value derived, and prune the remainder.

Over-investment in relationships will take precious time away from concentrating on your company's technological elements. Invest your time wisely in balancing consumer recognition needs, emerging technology, and future organizational strategy.

Strong relationship networks may often shut out new individuals and new thinking, insulating you from new feedback from the "outside." New insights, new experiences, and meaningful progress can be created by incorporating new elements into your network.

Overall, your relationship networks' scope and complexity are more important to your business success than your ability to identify and develop the ideal solution.

These partnerships motivate you to take chances confidently and actively, continuously innovate, and rebound along the way from defeats and setbacks. Your organization is a nation and not an island. You can't just run it.

How to develop good client relationships

Focusing their energies on gaining new business ideas is popular for independent professionals. New ventures don't necessarily mean new customers, however. Building and maintaining good relationships will set you up for repeat business with current customers. And even if your customers don't come back to you, they can suggest you to their colleagues.

Follow these six tips to create enduring relationships with your customers.

1. Emphasis on Unusual Contact

   A focus should be timely, effective contact. Communication with a single customer does not, of course, consistently and unreasonably violate your time or adversely affect your efficiency. Being available, however, shows that the project and satisfaction of your client are important to you.

   You can also establish a strong friendship, in addition to timely and detailed contact, by making your customers feel comfortable being transparent and frank with you. They should feel that they would take their ideas and concerns seriously.

2. Holding a good outlook

   You face many duties as an independent practitioner. As stressed out or exhausted as you can feel, it 's important for your clients to have a positive face. Exude the energy and trust you want your customers to feel about your job. Enthusiasm and enthusiasm are appealing personality characteristics that people enjoy being around and with which customers enjoy working.

3. Recognition of your client as a person

    If your relationship with your client is professional, it can go a long way to understand that you see them as an person, that is, more than just a paycheck. Depending on your business, customer type, and the personality of the individual customer, the degree to which this personal relationship is suitable can differ. You may simply ask how their kids are doing if you know your client is a mom. If you have a closer relationship with your customer, something more intimate might be fitting and appreciated, such as emailing them a news story about their favorite artist.

4. Share Expertise

    If your client does not understand your area of expertise, they may feel unaware of the process's intricacies and therefore disconnected from the project 's growth. This is your chance to exchange data that will help the customer understand what you do, which will create faith and trust in the process. It will make them feel informed and in-the-loop by explaining to your client what you did, why you did it, and how you came to your decision.

5. About your views, be open

    They must be able to trust and rely on you as an expert in order to build a strong and lasting relationship with customers. That is why, when it comes to your professional views and point of view on the best interests of the project, it is crucial to maintain a policy of openness. By telling a client what you think they want to hear or withholding your true opinion about their project, it can be tempting to want to appear agreeable and avoid uncomfortable confrontation.

However, not only are these practices counterproductive, but they can also harm your reputation, reducing your chances of a lasting relationship. Clients will respect your initiative and desire for excellence by confidently expressing your honest opinions.

6. Surpass expectations

One of the best ways to help build a strong customer relationship is to establish a reputation as an independent professional that delivers outstanding results. Make sure you're not overselling yourself and promising unrealistic outcomes. You allow yourself to completely impress the client with the final project and position yourself as someone with whom they would like to continue working by setting reasonable expectations.

Consider and determine what would be valuable to your client. It could be as easy as delivering the project in an aesthetically pleasing format, delivering the materials by hand and providing an in-depth walkthrough or demonstration, or including a small value-adding feature that improves the finished results. For loyal customers, a token of appreciation and thanks can be an unexpected pleasure that strengthens your professional relationship after key business milestones or around the holidays. The trick is to find the chance to go in a way that your customers can enjoy, above and beyond.

Chapter 6

HAVE COURAGE TO ACT CORRECTLY

Nobody can make decisions that are always right. However, many can act by taking into account the right guiding principles. These principles must be sought, found and applied scrupulously. They will allow us to be able to listen to ourselves and ask questions to ourselves, with the intent to understand how to act in certain situations and to live without the morbid fear that if fed leads to stalling and the impossibility of growth and improvement. The easiest way to overcome fear is to face it, not to experience it, to know how to control and manage it, so as not to live at the mercy of it, fueling insecurity and frustration, with the risk that it will kill our projects, our dreams, creativity, initiative, desire to test new projects, and determination. Fear exists, so let's use it as an ally, an energy that if well-managed leads to determination and self-confidence. Acting correctly, without wrong conditioning but accepting the right advice, is the only way that will lead us to the desired results.

Taking control of your life is only possible if you act correctly towards yourself, others and your business.

Stop wishing, start acting

This book is full of nuggets that will motivate, inspire, teach, challenge and encourage people to discard their wishing and embrace action to be able to take control of their life and achieve their life goals. Positive mind attracts positive result and a negative mind attracts negative result.

Courage as a skill

At the highest levels of his organization, a division blows the whistle on corruption. A young manager declines to work on the pet project of her employer because she believes the company would be discredited by it. A CEO urges his board to make a serious investment in environmentally friendly technologies despite pushing back from strong, aggressive members. In businesses around the world, such things happen every day. What is behind these high-risk acts, which are always brave?

We learned in 25 years of researching human behaviour in companies that bravery in business never functions like this. I've discovered that this kind of bravery is rarely impulsive from interviews with over 200 senior and mid-level managers who have behaved bravely, whether on behalf of society, their firms, their peers, or their professions. It's not coming from nowhere either.

In company, a special form of measured risk-taking is brave behavior. People who become successful leaders have a greater than average ability to make risky decisions, but with thorough deliberation and planning, they improve their chances of success and prevent career suicide. Business bravery is not so much the inborn trait of a visionary leader as an ability learned by decision-making processes of power that develop with practice. In other words, the majority of great business leaders train themselves to make choices at high risk. Over some period of time, sometimes decades, they learn to do this well.

It takes an understanding of what I call "courage calculation" to learn to take an intelligent gamble: a way to make success more possible while avoiding reckless, unproductive, or unreasonable actions. The courage measurement is made up of six distinct processes: setting primary and secondary goals; deciding the value of achieving them; tipping the power balance in your favor; balancing risks against benefits; choosing the best time for action and creating contingency plans.

Configuring goals

These questions are answered by the first component of the courage calculation: What does success in this high-risk situation look like? Are they obtainable? If my primary goal is organizational, does it defend the principles and values of my company or team or advance them? What is my secondary objective if I can't meet my primary goal?

Suppose they are about to fire a well-regarded colleague. He was maligned, and this was done by the person who poisoned his well to clear his route to promotion. A poor listener is the senior manager that will do the firing and tends to kill messengers. Should you try to save your coworker, given the politics?

Your goals should be reasonably within reach, whether primary or secondary, not pie-in-the-sky ambitions. A secondary organizational objective may be to determine the senior manager of a "mouse" in the midst of the business. A primary aim that directly serves you might be to gain some credit behind the scenes for supporting the employee. A secondary personal purpose might be to feel like you have done something for the public good.

While it would be difficult to estimate the chances of success until the other decisions in the courage equation have been made, it is possible to think about the probability of primary-goal achievement at this stage.

Determining the value of your objectives

These questions are answered in the second part of the courage calculation: How necessary is it for you to achieve your aim or objectives? Is the business going to suffer if you don't do anything about the current state of affairs? Can they derail your career? Will the situation call for more complex and less dangerous urgent, high-profile intervention or something? Courage is not a matter of squandering political resources on matters of low priority.

Will the situation call for more complex and less dangerous urgent, high-profile intervention or something? Courage is not a matter of squandering political resources on matters of low priority.

Spear-in-the-sand circumstances require you to weigh your confidence in the cause against the risks involved. These cases are rare: they arise when it is difficult or impossible to compromise, flexible minds are difficult to find, and doing nothing is simply not an option.

Tipping the balance of power

In organizations, people sometimes believe that control is a simple matter of location on the organizational map. Many individuals prefer never to take a stand while trying to appease those above them. But in fact, even those in top management offer power to everyone on whom they rely, whether for respect, guidance, friendship, appreciation, or association with the network. Seen in this sense, authority is something we have tremendous power over. For example, you gain sway over individuals who otherwise hold sway over you by developing relationships with and influencing those around you. This gives you a wider foundation to make bold moves from. You can form supportive power networks wisely in advance, but it takes time to develop them.

Choosing the proper time

Strong leaders have an uncanny sense of timing as well. "The real leader knows" when to make compromises, when to negotiate, when to use the art of losing the fight to win the battle.

It can be argued that the issue of timing should be insignificant when someone is faced with a situation that needs bravery. We believe that courageous people may not hesitate to act in spear-in-the-sand circumstances when something is at stake and emotions are running high. In emergencies, this may be true, but a single-minded rush to action in business is typically foolish.

Consider what happened when, a year before he was able to do so, one group of senior managers forced their CEO, who was in his seventies, to create a succession plan. He was profoundly hurt by the CEO, who had always treated his managers like family. Although he did not reject the idea of succession planning, he found it premature and impertinent to push it. The CEO later told me, had the managers waited, they would have accomplished their goal. Yet they have been stubborn. The rage of the CEO grew; he edged one manager out, and soon the others were searching for new jobs.

While emotion is still in the mix, and when making a brave move can also be an advantage, the following questions can help to calculate objectively whether the time is right:

- Why am I now doing this?
- Am I considering an action or an impulsive one considered?
- How long does it take to train yourself better? It's too long for that?
- What are the benefits and disadvantages of waiting for a day, two days, a week or more?
- What are the barriers to politics? Can they be either eliminated or temporarily reduced?
- Can I take action now that will later build the basis for a brave move?
- Am I prepared emotionally and mentally to take this risk?
- Do I have the experience to make this work, communication skills, track record, and credibility?

Of course, spending too much time on any or all of these problems will lead you into the pit of Hamlet, and the chance for bravery will pass you by. At the same time, an o'er-hasty leap can result from too little thought. It is important to note that in industry, brave action is mostly deliberative. True emergencies are uncommon. Time might well be on the side of you.

For the most part, courageous behaviour in business is deliberative. True emergencies are uncommon. Time might well be on the side of you.

Marshaling sufficient help, information, or evidence to enhance your chances of success is crucial before you make your move.

Research suggests that there is an instinct for opportunity for those who behave courageously in business settings. They easily read circumstances, but they are never reckless. They pause, reflect, and consider another time or route if they feel that the emotional environment is not right for a frontal attack, or that history or politics poses insurmountable obstacles. They continue to collect their energy and wait for a more propitious moment if they feel outmatched or lack the ability or endurance to go the distance. The most challenging aspect of the courage calculation is finding the right time; it requires a deep sensitivity to one's surroundings and a great deal of flexibility.

Developing arrangements for contingency

Faced with having to take a chance, most individuals make only one attempt: they ring the doorbell, and they give up and go away if an answer is not forthcoming. Many who fulfill their primary and secondary objectives continue to knock on the back door, knock on a window, or even return a second time.

In dangerous circumstances, winning also involves being something you haven't been, thinking like you didn't think, and behaving like you haven't acted. The more your contingency plans are made, the more likely it is that you can achieve your primary and secondary objectives. But it's important to account for potential failure before determining how to proceed with your decision-making capacity. If you don't achieve your goal, then what? Is the squad going to lose credibility? You going to think about resigning? If not, how would you be able to save your work or your reputation? Is it possible to turn failure into something positive?

Contingency training is just about creativity. People who take bold risks and excel are versatile thinkers; alternate routes are prepared for them.

Courageous administrators plan themselves, including worst-case scenarios, for any eventuality.

Ultimately, company bravery is based on goals that represent a personal, corporate, or social philosophy. When this philosophy is supported by clear, achievable primary and secondary objectives and evaluation of their significance, a favorable power base, a thorough risk-benefit assessment, adequate timing, and well-developed contingency plans, managers are better empowered to make bold moves that serve their organizations, their careers, and their sense of personal value.

How can the world be changed by an act of courage?

Courage in someone who experiences the act will instill a positive feeling. The positive feeling is infectious and, by rippling out into ever-widening circles, changes the world. An act of bravery catapults humanity and every "growth spurt" we have collectively encountered has precipitated it.

Truly, mankind can be empowered by a brave act far more than is lost in one human life. Thus, the martyrs whose lives have driven the spiritual growth of mankind.

It gives you strength to be deeply loved by others, while loving someone deeply gives you courage. It is understated and profound, the strength of love to offer courage.

Behind every brave act is love.

Every brave act in which a mortal has walked through his fears for the good of something greater than himself, including the martyr, has paid tremendous dividends to humanity.

For what he believes, every man gives his life. For what she believes, every woman gives her life. Sometimes people believe in little or nothing, so they give little or nothing of their lives. One life is all we have, and we live it as we believe in living it ... and then it's gone.

But it's more awful than dying to surrender who you are and to live without belief-even more awful than dying young.

May we love each other with purity and tenacity, so that we can add faith and bravery to every human being we encounter.

How to act appropriately with your bravery

Courage is not fear's absence. Courageous people feel fear, however their fear can be controlled and resolved, so that they do not avoid taking action.

They also use fear to ensure that they are not overly optimistic and that the necessary steps are taken. How are they doing this? Instead of handling them, they taught themselves to control their emotional reaction to fear so that they manage it. How you can learn to do this is set out on this page.

What is courage?

Courage is a highly-prized attribute, and over the years, many prominent and valued individuals have spoken or written about it. We all certainly have an understanding of what we mean by courage, or as it is often called, bravery.

Courageous individuals stand up to things that harm them, or the things they care about, or the people they care about. In a way that is compatible with their beliefs, they take action. The action needed often, however, is not necessarily loud, but quiet and reflective.

The other view that bravery is always taken is that it takes real risk to be taken, but with consideration.

Courage and being courageous is not about jumping in blindly, but worrying about it and then, if possible, doing it anyway.

The advantages of courage

Generally, behaving courageously makes one feel comfortable because it includes feelings being mastered.

The very fact that we celebrate bravery so much shows us that this is an activity that is very human. Courage can also motivate us to do 'positive' things in the sense of behaving in a way that reacts to danger appropriately, not over-confidently or in a cowardly way.

Courage also encourages us to behave against those who attack, or who behave badly. For itself, the Western world has historically respected bravery; if courage is displayed, achievement is not required.

Courage controls and overcomes anxiety and unnecessary trust.

In general, anxiety and overconfidence are perceived as negative emotions. They make us, either at the time or afterwards, feel bad.

Fear is closely related to life, like many emotions.

We are afraid of things that threaten our life, and an adrenaline reaction (which normally means that we are motivated to 'fight' or 'flight') controls our response. Adrenaline's physical effects include freezing, clammy skin, as the blood is diverted from the vital organs to allow you to run away quickly, the feeling of 'butterflies' in the stomach, shivering or shaking, and even chattering teeth.

When you are worried that you will not survive anything, being afraid tells you. Your emotional reaction cannot be logical, though, as our page on Controlling Emotions points out. It's almost definitely correlated with memory, maybe an event, or something that you may have read.

Questions to ask yourself to put into action bravery include:

- What am I scared of?

  Is this the right thing to be terrified of?

  Should I fear it — or rationally, should I fear it less or more?

  What harm to me or anyone will this thing do?

What are the things that could arise because of my acts and/or inactions?

As a consequence of my acts and/or inactions, what is the worst that might happen?

- What are the threats to others and me?

  Courage gives us the power to measure an emotional reaction (fear) and to behave rationally and correctly.

  Over-Confidence Takeover

  Trust is healthy, trust gives us the power to act on our values, have faith in ourselves or others, and take action. However, over-confidence suggests that we might be too quick to take action and take needless risks.

  Since it's a really optimistic feeling, over-confidence is harder to recognize than fear. Esteem feels good, and over-confidence often does so. We do not feel afraid, since the risks of taking care of our lives have not been adequately measured.

Questions to ask yourself to better recognize and conquer over-confidence include:

- What do I think I should do?

  How would what I'm doing make a difference?

  How do I know that it would impact my actions? How can I be sure they're not going to do any damage?

Rationally, and not with bravado, answering these questions will help you decide whether you feel rightly optimistic or over-confident.

The two sides of the same coin are apprehension and over-confidence.

It is important to know whether you appear to suffer from fear or over-confidence so that you can focus on how to resolve that vulnerability, make sure you act bravely, and either not be overcome by your fears or take unnecessary risks because of over-confidence.

A balance discovery

In comparison to either timidity or cockiness / over-confidence, displaying courage is all about striking the right balance, which means that you'll need to think about it beforehand.

Ultimately, the question to ask yourself is, perhaps:

How will I feel getting to know how this end? Would I believe that I have behaved in accordance with my values?

If yes is your answer to the question or that it is compatible with your principles, that's a good way to behave.

On the other hand, if you're worried about feeling like you're going to 'run away' or 'have been a little careless,' then you may want to think about alternate acts.

Chapter 7

WANTING AND KNOWING HOW TO CHANGE OURSELVES AND OUR HABITS

A few simple words, but which open infinite possibilities. "Wanting and knowing how to change ourselves" implies the will first. Everything starts from the personal will of transformation, from that first inner step that projects us from a known world to yet another to be discovered. The will to change ourselves is the spring that, if well managed, will allow us to act towards a better chance. What is closely linked to the excellent potential of positive "will" is the unique and irreplaceable basis of "knowledge". There cannot be a true and correct will to change without equally fair and adequate knowledge. This is why it is essential not only to "want to change ourselves" but also to know how to do it: "to know how to change ourselves". This is the key that will allow you to test new ideas, wanting and knowing how to do it, and thus take control of your life.

Often what keeps us anchored to the routine of our life is the sad force of habit. Habits are one of the strongest enemies with which we must clash for our personal growth because they give us what we daily seek as a fundamental need: safety. But instead of looking for it in ourselves, security, badly managed or wrong habits lead us to look for it in others and in aspects external to us, which may be wrong or may disappear over time. That's why the advice we are given is: "transform your habits". So try to do things differently than you are used to, explore new possibilities, access new information, test new ideas and develop new thought patterns. If we seek security and find it within ourselves, we will wear something that nothing or nobody can ever take away from us. The power of habit will be a formidable weapon only when we learn to manage it properly and only when it leads us to correct and useful actions. Getting out of the vortex of habits consolidated over time will help us develop a more elastic and flexible mentality, have strong decision-making power and will free us from personal insecurities and psychological dependencies that prevent us from making ourselves progress and consequently our business.

You must be a person in continuous transformation, growth and improvement, seizing and taking advantage of every opportunity and every opportunity, because it is a fundamental feature to be able to take control of your life.

Changing habit: Hacks to change your life

"We are what we repeatedly do. And be aware that excellence then is not an act, but a habit." So true! I think that if we all took one bad habit that we see in ourselves and work on creating a new more positive habit to replace that bad habit we could work towards bettering our lives which in part ripples out and affects others.

My mother reminded me not that long ago about the "Butterfly effect" and I Googled it to refresh my memory on what it was about. A brief explanation of the theory behind it is, a small change in one person could and will set off a chain affecting others around them which in turn affects others and so on.

Ok, so for example: if half of the leaders in the world started focusing on being at peace within themselves and their families, then peace would start forming around them in other parts of their lives that would affect their people, countries, the rest of the leaders, and world.

Mother Teresa said it very well, "I never attend war rallies, but if you have a peace rally, I will be there". She lived the "Butterfly effect" daily because she changed so many people's lives just by living her own.

With being conscious of the "Butterfly effect" in your life, wouldn't you want to start changing your habits? A habit is created by doing the same thing every day for 28 days. If you see anything that you do in your life that you wish you could change, it starts with your thoughts. "Change your thoughts, change your life". So to change a bad habit then find a more positive, affirming habit to create and do it instead for 28 days straight. It is that easy! The hardest part of doing this is the thought process. You HAVE to change the way you think and believe in what you are thinking and wanting.

I know that for me I made a list of things, like a pros and cons list but calling it good and bad habits. Once I made that list, I looked at what I wanted to make better in my life and looked at my list of "bad" habits and said, "Ok, this habit only makes this and this in my life, but if I change this habit and do this instead then this part of my life would improve." I had to then think of all the reasons why I wanted to improve that area of my life. If my reasons were valid and real enough for me then I would be able to come up with a list of thoughts that would help me to get focused on changing my habit. Once I went through that process then the daily focus of creating a new habit would then become easier. Not easy, but easier because it was what I wanted and a "must-have" in my life.

By changing your thoughts, habits and life, you will affect others around you and change them too. The "Butterfly effect" really works and is a wonderful, blessed way to make the world a better place for us all. Take time today to see what you want to be changed in your life, what goal you have set and struggle to fulfil, or habit you want to change, and you will find you on your way to changing the world tomorrow. Remember "do or do not, there is no try" as a little green Jedi once told young Skywalker, so you might as well "Just Do It" ~ Nike.

How to change ourselves and succeed

Have you wondered why, over and over again, you make some of the same mistakes? Have you ever struggled with being effective? Have you ever wanted to know if there are any tricks and secrets that can make you go over-the-top completely?

You will always have what you have unless you change who you are. We will speak today about how we can improve ourselves in order to become more effective. For this to happen, there are three methods that we need to do. One, set targets. Two, be diligent, and number three, provide a curriculum for personal growth. You'll be able to resolve the challenges and become more competitive if you put this into motion.

Let 's start off. One, set targets.

Did you know that there are no fixed targets for 90% of all individuals? 5% of all individuals have set goals, but they do not accomplish them, which causes a lot of anger. And the last 5% goes to those people who set goals, write them down, and make their dreams come true. Many of the planet's motivational speakers talk about setting goals. Objectives are what make things possible. Goals are what make you excel. You'll fail to be mediocre at best without them.

Now, I'm not going to talk about how today's priorities should be set. There are several good programs for goal-setting, including my own. But today, I just want to emphasize that setting goals is crucial. Set and write down your objectives. When you write it down, there's power. It makes it real to write it down, makes it concrete, and will improve the chances of success. It goes from opportunity to reality.

That brings us to our second proactive move. The benefit of being proactive. It is a foundational practice to be proactive. Of all the seven behaviors, the main one is this. The others are all standing on this one right here.

Being proactive means deciding how to respond. Choices are offered to us. We can either choose to be positive or to be negative. The collection is ours. Have you ever found that these ineffective people are reactive in our lives? Anything happens that doesn't quite go their way, so they blow up. They're exploding. They're making the situation worse.

We have to admit, sometimes, that we respond the same way. But that way, we don't have to be. We're able to choose how to respond. We should allow our logic and our beliefs to direct our feelings. There are positive feelings, but they are chaotic. Emotions are good, but not always consistent. Let your logic on how to solve the situation and your principles on what you think is right lead the way. It's not easy, but the constructive ones are the most effective individuals.

So, we are committed to setting targets and writing them down. We prefer to be constructive instead of reactive. That takes us to our third step, which is to provide a program for personal growth.

What puts you over the top is getting a professional improvement program. That's exactly what a curriculum for personal growth is supposed to do. It's about constantly improving ourselves.

Today I've got a very easy idea for you. Here it is: In whatever area you want to improve yourself in, read one book a month. It's that. Read one monthly book. Now, if you read the book, listen to the audio book, or get an audio / video program on the subject, I don't care.

Research tells us that if we stick to this challenge, we will be in the top 5 percent of the world 's experts in that particular field in five years. Strong, that is. But it also shows us how few individuals are willing to do it. You will be shocked at your success if you take this opportunity and dedicate yourself to this program, and you will not recognize yourself one year from now.

So, you've got it there. Three quick steps to succeed and transform yourself. One, setting priorities. Two, make the decision to be proactive. Three, a program for personal growth. If you take these three steps to take action, you will improve yourself ... and succeed. Go out there now and make it happen.

Research says making new rituals and sticking to them before they become patterns is the best way to incorporate change into your life.

The way to make sure that the new behaviour is cultivated is to reward ourselves. We repeat the action again and again with inspiration, until it becomes entrenched.

However, here are some useful steps that you can take along the way:

1. Find a reason in what you do. Purpose drives sense. You're inspired to make something better because you have a goal and you think it will make a positive difference in the world.
2. Your amygdala, stop listening. In the center of your brain, the amygdala, an almond-shaped piece, is in charge of keeping you safe. But it gets in the way of you taking brave measures and moving with confidence occasionally. The next time you're scared of doing something, do it anyway — your amygdala's just doing its work.
3. Cultivate fantastic experiences. Relationships are often depicted by magic as maintaining themselves, but they take time and effort in practice. Think of them as an investment that develops with the patience, care, and appreciation of constant deposits.
4. Build your mental endurance. What? How? Anytime you find yourself criticizing someone, taking it all too seriously, or giving in to distraction, stop yourself. Avoid blaming the past or external variables for the decisions that you make.
5. Make a good listener of yourself. One of the keys to building resilience and preserving equilibrium in your life is good communication. It's the basis on which our lives are founded, the way we understand others and encourage them to know and understand us. And listening is fundamental to communication — the most significant ability we possess, arguably.
6. Oh, support others. Getting out of your mind is one of the best antidotes to stress, and the best way to distract yourself is by helping someone else. When you are busy caring for others, you cannot think for yourself.

7. Only ask questions. Curiosity is among the best abilities that you can create. In particular, curiosity about individuals enriches the business networks. Interact with and draw others out. You're going to learn wonderful stuff and develop a reputation as a great conversationalist.
8. Alone, carve out some time. For some of us, it's easier to do than others, but a certain amount of time alone allows for a happy and productive existence. The lack of private time is a big cause of unhappiness. Look for ways to give yourself a few lonely moments.
9. Keep a Journal of Thanks. Grateful feelings lead to keeping pessimism and concern at bay. Numerous studies have linked appreciation, satisfaction with life, and optimism to greater happiness.
10. Take an opportunity. Risks may be daunting, but the things we didn't take a chance on are more likely to regret than the things we did. Practice taking intelligent risks — that is, risks associated with something important to you.
11. Learn something new. It doesn't matter which area or how easy or hard it is. The mind is recharged by new learning and helps you feel more competent.
12. Get your workspace great. Your atmosphere can have a significant impact on your efficiency and effectiveness. Experiment with making your office one that is perfect for the tasks you do and a position you enjoy spending time in.

Chapter 8

KNOWING HOW TO DREAM IN A PROGRAMMED WAY

The dream, linked to that need to desire something other than what you are or have, has always been evaluated from two different angles and consequently has two corresponding judgments. The negative and the positive one. Dreaming for the sake of dreaming can bring a lightness of mind as disastrous consequences, for this reason, it is right to face this issue correctly and not superficially, but deeply. The dream is one of the strongest fuels that man has to take his steps. The problem with the dream is that, regardless of whether it is the right one or not, or whether it is correct or not, he still moves us. The first action, therefore, is to identify the correct, useful and ideal dreams for our purposes, and to pursue those. The central pivot of our efforts must be to know how to manage our time well in the search and pursuit of dreams useful for our life and the well-being of those around us. When everything in our life has the right balance, even our business will have its right space, but we will be able to manage it, not him! This is a source of real decision-making power.

Even this chapter rests the whole reasoning on the verb "to know" because it is at the basis of the success of true dreams, and it is only knowing "what" to dream and "how" to do it that one can achieve the dreams so desired. For a dream to come true, chasing it is not enough, there is a need for an action plan. In other words, daydreaming in the positive sense of the term. Once the dream to be understood is understood, it is essential to establish the actions to be carried out in the short and long term, writing them down perhaps by points, and planning the dates by which to reach these intermediate objectives, until the ultimate goal is achieved. Seeing how over time the steps we take are carried out from time to time will give us the energy necessary to continue towards the new steps of the program, so our dream one step at a time will be ever closer and achievable. So, take control of your life also on this fundamental aspect, it will be useful to make many of your dreams come true, including what will lead you to achieve your business.

Test New Ideas, Both In Business And In Interpersonal Relationships

"Change" does not mean zeroing ourselves and starting from scratch. Not only is it wrong, but it's also not possible, our correct thoughts and ways of doing do and will continue to be part of our lives. Even if we do not want them, the changes will still take place, and it is for this reason that we must be able to transform a simple and normal change into real improvement. The only way forward is to test new ideas and believe in them, change that part of yourself that slows down the process of growth and improvement, those patterns of thought or behaviour that in different situations still create always identical results. One way to start this process is to take time to study and meditate on your mistakes and learn from them never to repeat them.

Today many of them are born in the world and many of them die, but in this case, as in many other similar situations, failure is experience, knowledge of your sector and opportunities to create new successful initiatives and thus test new ideas. The choice to test new ideas, both in business and in interpersonal relationships, is fundamental to guarantee a progressive positive trend of life and the experiences connected to them, either personal or working.

How to test your new business ideas?

You've got a brilliant idea and you're excited to immerse yourself in entrepreneurship. But, are you certain that your idea is viable? You need to test your idea's true potential before investing in a new venture.

However, failure is a normal part of business; however, the majority of us are not equipped to "fail efficiently."

This helps in avoiding catastrophic failures that can lead to personal and financial ruin. Christensen says that during skiing, one does not take his or her skis and point them directly down the mountain because this will result in a severe disaster.

Instead of bulldozing your way towards a specific goal, slow down and alter your course. This process helps achieve success, and if there is a failure, the business fails "efficiently".

Here are some ways to test your business concept with target clients:

Have a focus group: A focus group includes a select number of customers who use and provide input on your products. Before you go all in, focus groups, polls, and interviews demonstrate what customers think.

Ask social media groups: Your target market is put at your fingertips by the internet. Find groups online that might be interested in your business. Find out their general impressions and you can do something differently if they think you should.

Set up a page for crowdfunding: Websites for crowdfunding give more than just investors. You may also receive useful reactions from like-minded citizens, insights, and suggestions. Bonus: you could meet someone who wants your idea to be invested in.

Testing the concept on a small group reveals whether customers care about your deals. There's a fair chance your idea would be a hit with a wider audience if the small market tests are successful.

To test your new business ideas, here are 8 tips.

1. Ask the correct questions

For your business venture, unclear ideas and partial plans would likely trigger a rough start. You must ask yourself the correct questions to get the answers you need.

Next, take every element of your start-up into account. The questions you ask should help you dig deeper into the process of your thinking and create a strategy. Resolving problems, in the beginning, will help you succeed.

Before you start a company, these questions are examples of what you should think about:

Why do I want a company to be started?

- What problem am I solving?
- Who is my main customer?
- What tools do I have?
- What are my objectives?

In a journal, you should write down your replies to solidify your feelings. You can start the next steps in testing your business concept as soon as you answer general questions.

2. Know the rivals

You don't want to get too wrapped up with what you do with your rivals. But, knowing their methods is a good thing. Analyze businesses similar to yours before launching your start-up.

You can see what has succeeded in the past by looking at other firms. From others that have already attempted similar concepts, a wise business owner discovers. Because of a failed plan, you gain valuable insights without suffering any losses.

It will also help you identify what makes your idea stand out by evaluating the competition. You need to show customers how special your company is in order to get a strong customer base. This could be anything from disrupting the market with a new product to delivering an experience that is exclusive.

3. Assess the money

We've all heard the saying, 'It takes money to make it.' For a reason, the expression has become a cliche-it's accurate in most cases. To get your start-up off the ground, you will need business capital.

It is likely that start-up funding comes from many sources. Many entrepreneurs finance the expense of starting a new business with personal assets, such as a credit card or a savings account. And others reach out to friends around them for support, also their family. For small businesses, banks and private lenders also sell loan services.

Chances are, to finance your company, you will need a mix of capital solutions. Since you have not yet developed yourself as a viable company, it could be difficult to secure start-up funds. Create a small business plan to persuade people that your project is feasible, which sets out how you are going to spend the money and how much you hope to gain.

4. Test the demand

Your target market is one of the best outlets for checking the business concept. Define the dream client and concentrate on who is going to be involved in your offerings. Then, do a small group's business research.

5. Care about profitability first

The first advice is to think about profitability first while evaluating your new business ideas. Christensen advises that by concentrating on profitability, new projects begin. He goes on to say that even if there is a small diversion from the overall goal, think of the fastest ways to profitability. Devoting 65 percent of the capital to the profitability goal, 25 percent to resources such as employees, and 10 percent to scale, while deciding on a pre-fixed amount of resources that you are willing to risk as part of the business venture, whether it is a new business idea or business.

6. Ensuring the effectiveness of failure

If profits are not earned within a pre-determined time frame, a new business idea is a failure. He calls this failure an effective failure, though. The time frame for success will differ from business to business depending on how much investment you're ready to make in your venture. Some entrepreneurs will spend years staring at losses before quitting.

7. Concentrate on your priorities

The business venture proceeds towards, after earning income, which includes the allocation of 65% of resources to personnel, processes, and procedures, 25% to scale (through franchising or expansion), and 10% to profitability. This method should continue to use this model of resource allocation that rotates during the company's tenure across capital, size, and profitability.

8. The Slow Down

You have to admit that it would take a longer period of time for companies that follow the zig-zag concept to meet their objectives. He goes on to say that projects can be more stable and the decrease in pace can give rise to fun surprises by setting clear-cut targets when it comes to people, time, and money in the company venture.

A considerable amount of risk is associated with new business ideas. Budding entrepreneurs will taste sweet success within a short period of time with the right strategy and the right preparation.

Adopting new strategic concepts for company development

Especially when it comes to introducing new business ideas, there is a need to come up with sound business management practices for your business to succeed. Even before they were tested, many company owners were known to squash on fresh business ideas. They argue that the principles have been attempted elsewhere and failed.

Since the organization may have other goals, managers take this as an excuse to neglect the latest business ideas or place them on hold only because they do not support them. Strong business management calls for the efficient and proper assessment of new concepts to be placed in motion.

Managers need to provide processes that better assist in testing and trying new strategies at minimum costs in order for business development to occur. To find out whether they are worth the try, these ideas have to be quickly tested. You need to know the value of reasoning management as a business manager so that no good idea goes to waste and, when appropriate, decisive action is taken.

Creative business management takes into account the challenges inherent in implementing innovative concepts and that these ideas will yield positive results with suitable techniques. As a company owner should learn how to understand them, new business developments are not accepted or promoted.

When you do not jump into a new business idea, it may sound like you are playing it safe, but the downside is seeing the same idea that you missed when your competitor introduced it. Instead of stamping on new ideas, processes are put in place to test, introduce and even reward people who come up with these ideas.

Introduction of interpersonal relationship building

A close connection between people working together in the same company refers to an interpersonal relationship. Colleagues working together should share a special bond so that they can better achieve their level. For a healthy interpersonal relationship and ultimately a productive environment at work, individuals need to be frank with each other.

The interpersonal relationships that you develop at work are a vital piece of the overall workplace puzzle, with managers and colleagues, or any of your suppliers, and can directly influence your work success and career development.

You'll learn in this book:

- Tips for interpersonal relationship management

Different forms of management / leadership and how to achieve in each of them

How to identify different kinds of troublesome coworkers and how to communicate with them

Why are interpersonal experiences significant?

In both your work success and career development, interpersonal relationships that you form at work play a critical role. Good communication and understanding among colleagues can be made possible by positive interpersonal relationships.

Make sure that the direction of your management team is supported by what you do and how you work. Know, before you learn how to become a good assistant, you cannot become a good leader. Show your colleagues / managers that you are a "unit member."

Here are a few methods that you can use to help make your manager (and colleagues) aware that you are dependable and confident in your abilities:

- Show respect.
- Give your best.
- Be honest.
- Keep lines of communication open.
- Maintain boundaries.
- Be positive.
- Manage your emotions.
- Be open to feedback.

An important part of job satisfaction is healthy relationships in the workplace. You will note a rise in efficiency and overall job satisfaction when developing relationships in the workplace. You will create enduring, professional relationships by taking some steps towards knowing your emotional intelligence and getting to know your coworkers. In this article, we address the advantages of establishing relationships in the workplace, as well as practical steps you should take when creating your own.

What are in-workplace relationships?

The experiences you have with your colleagues are relationships in the workplace. You are more likely to enjoy your daily life when you have effective relationships with other professionals and team members. For career success, building relationships in the workplace is also critical. Relationships with peers in the workplace not only help with networking, but they can also provide you with the support and motivation you need to excel in your job. The following advantages are provided by workplace relations:

- Increased contentment with your work
- Enhanced convenience for reports and team meetings
- Enhanced productivity for all members of the team
- Moral reinforcement and aid in meeting tough deadlines
- Higher rates of retention

Elements of healthy relationships within the workplace

Understanding the components of a healthy relationship in the workplace will help you evaluate your own relationships and recognise the areas in which you want to change. Healthy relationships in the workplace tend to have the following features:

Confidence: When developing a working relationship, the ability to trust your peers and the feeling that you can count on them is an significant trait.

Acceptance: An essential factor is acceptance and appreciation of each other and your role in the relationship in the workplace.

Team member: People who work together in a team environment tend to have better relationships, doing their fair share of the job and providing credit where it is due.

Open communication: For every partnership, including a workplace one, open communication is essential. One of the first steps towards a working relationship is to promote open communication, to ask questions and to get to know your colleagues.

How to establish workplace relationships

It can naturally come to others to create positive relationships in the workplace. However, you can use the following steps even if you are unsure how to turn co-worker relationships into productive relationships in the workplace:

- Understand your weaknesses and strengths
- To build relationships, plan time
- Ask and listen to questions
- Provide assistance
- Know when to ask for help
- Appreciate the position of each employee

- Maintain your obligations

Be present, be present,

1. Understand your weaknesses and strengths

It can be important to consider the strengths and weaknesses before working on the growth of new workplace relationships. When initiating workplace relationships, learning relationship skills such as communication, active listening and dispute resolution will benefit you. Review the good qualities you bring to a new relationship in the workplace and consider the things in a relationship you like. Assessing your emotional intelligence (EI) will help with this assignment. Knowing your emotional intelligence requires reflecting on:

- Self-awareness: Self-awareness is the power, in your profession and in a relationship, to be mindful of your own needs and desires.

- Self-regulation: By having your long-term objectives in mind, self-regulation is the ability to control your own feelings and thoughts.

- Empathy: Empathy is the capacity to understand and empathize with the condition of another person.

- Social skills: When forming new relationships, the development of essential social skills such as teamwork, conflict resolution, communication and problem-solving skills are critical.

2. To build relationships, plan time

In the workplace, creating healthy relationships requires time. Your position 's regular demands and responsibilities will make it hard to find time to connect with other members of the team. You can find it easier to connect with and get to know your colleagues by arranging time to establish relationships. During lunch, during the first 10 minutes of your workday or when you leave the office at the end of the day, you might schedule time. You might also arrange a meeting's first 10 minutes to be a moment where everybody catches up with each other. Furthermore, many companies have after-work trips or team activities that can be perfect for building relationships in the workplace.

3. Ask and listen to questions

Asking questions and listening actively would not only encourage you to learn more about your colleagues, but it is also an vital part of the relationship building process. You demonstrate an interest in them when you ask questions about your coworker's personal life, professional ambitions or everyday needs. Before sharing your own, give them the chance to share information about their lives. Often, your colleagues may come to equate you with becoming a successful communicator by asking questions and promoting open communication. For complaints, celebrations or when they just need someone to listen, they are more likely to come to you.

4. Provide assistance

A perfect way to develop a partnership is to take the pressure away from a coworker while they are struggling to complete a project. If you know a coworker is stressed and you have a couple of spare minutes, consider offering them support. Confidence is an important part of building relationships and you are illustrating this quality by supporting colleagues when they need it most.

5. Know when to ask for help

Asking for support may also start a friendship in the workplace. You have more opportunities to get to know them by inviting colleagues to join in on projects or job tasks. Often, bear in mind that since you have previously provided the same assistance to others, you are more likely to obtain the assistance you need. Relationships include both give and take, and by asking for and providing assistance, you can show this.

6. Appreciate the position of each employee

Appreciation is a strong constructor of relationships. Sometimes, the problems of another department can seem difficult to grasp and tensions may lead to negative feelings. You will understand the particular position of each employee with the company by keeping in mind that each department has distinct objectives. It can be helpful to come up with solutions to a dilemma rather than jumping to conclusions or putting the blame. You will find that you develop a new sense of respect for your colleagues by working together in a constructive and professional manner, which will help you to start building a healthy relationship.

7. Maintain your obligations

The act of sustaining your commitments is to further build on faith. When your colleagues or team members know that they know that they can count on you, you are more likely to establish better relationships. If you find it difficult to maintain commitments due to a busy work schedule, inform colleagues that when they request your presence, you will need to get back to them. When agreeing to job commitments or future activities, please be practical.

8. In the office, be there

It can always feel like the day flies by, with the many tasks and demands that come with the workday. Multi-tasking during the day, answering emails during a team meeting or working on your report during lunch can feel more productive. These duties, however, keep you from being present. You will find that you are able to develop working relationships with minimal effort by paying attention to those around you, starting contact and getting to know your colleagues.

Do your share of this job. Volunteering to take on tough tasks. Incorporate fun games and icebreakers into team projects so that participants are better able to know each other. Be an encourager by celebrating others' achievements and encouraging them to do more.

Communicate well by listening clearly and speaking

Develop your communication skills by listening and communicating clearly to others attentively. Echo the sentence in your own terms if you are not sure that you understand the other person, and ask if you understand it correctly. Let others know that their views are respected by you. During talks, maintain eye contact.

Keep your feelings under control, and if anything upsets you, don't use berating expressions. Provide consumers, service providers and other professionals with your calling card so that they can reach you.

Be considerate of others

Demonstrate consideration for others. Be knowledgeable in other employees' viewpoints, and be able to discuss points of view that are different from your own. In a courteous way, share your own viewpoints. Avoid sharing long personal stories and sending unrelated job emails.

Limit personal phone calls and distractions, such as radios, if you work in a shared office room. Maintain an attitude of professional and courteous.

One of the most critical aspects of getting a job done is relationship building. Many individuals have a lot of knowledge and abilities, but you might lose their valuable perspectives if you do not establish a relationship.

Constructing partnerships on the road is even more important. You have a short time to establish a working relationship with that. So be proactive about a good relationship being established.

Take advantage of the office's time abroad. Two computer screens and stacks of paper are not all relationships constructed. In order to get to know the individual, use your relaxing time. Ask them a question or two about what they want in life, and you're going to have an all-toe chat.

Many business people go to a bar or club to contact them. Yet you must be alert to religious and cultural taboos. It can seem to be just the place to unwind for you. But your emotions need to be put on hold and do what's best for your relationship.

Drinking might just be a hot button. Like soldiers or Americans, some cultures do not prefer alcohol. Several religions have stringent rules concerning temperance. So be careful not to insult yourself. Simply questioning is the best policy.

To take your touch out to a fancy restaurant if it might be more convenient for you. This works generally well. But often from some loud mouth jerk who makes offensive remarks, you find yourself at the next table over. This does not encourage you to talk about sensitive problems.

Know that you can still take them home for dinner with your mom. Here, the challenge is to keep it professional. In the eyes of your contact, you want to create a relationship, not to become another jerk.

Make sure that you talk about the menu, in any event. If you don't like your friend's salad, don't buy one for him. Talking about stuff like this goes a long way towards creating a relationship full of trust.

The majority of executives typically face the same dilemma. Their subordinates do not have a successful relationship with them. They face obstacles in engaging with individuals and they find it difficult to deal with conflict. In order to make matters smooth, they do not know how to deal with their workers. Will there be something done to make things better?

Of course, indeed. Seriously speaking, it is important to have a good personal relationship between supervisors and subordinates. It makes it better and quicker to pass items. It helps to improve the productivity of the job. At the same time, it allows everybody to build a happier working environment. If a manager develops near working relationships with both internal and external clients, he or she will undoubtedly achieve further career development merits.

The very first thing you need to have is a good mindset in order to strengthen working relationships with others. Typically, people with a good outlook look at things from a positive viewpoint and are confident about meeting all types of difficulties in their workplace. Moreover, in welcoming suggestions and criticism, they are more open-minded. They are able to develop their skills further by taking positive comments from distinct individuals. No matter how daunting the exercises are, they are able to overcome the issues quickly.

It is necessary to have faith in others to maintain successful relationships at work. It is a kind of reverence. You give your workers a new assignment, for instance, and you have full faith in him or her to complete the task. In return, since you trust his or her ability to carry out the job, he or she will put more effort into getting things accomplished. In the other hand, if you don't trust staff, you'll be curious about what people are doing, which would deter workers from putting 100 % effort into it.

It's not difficult to maintain a personal relationship at work. It does not require any private appointments or dating. Communication is the principal concern here. Do supervisors and subordinates have strong channels of communication? Here, I don't mean emails and memos. The best form of contact is not to send and receive emails. Based on various circumstances, we need to apply both formal and informal communication. You will be able to increase the progress of the job by staying in contact with each other regularly.

To sum up, it takes a lot of effort to develop successful personal relationships at work. If you are unfriendly and you are unable to devote all of your energy to work, don't expect people to be kind to you. In order to understand people better, you should take a constructive approach.

Have you ever wondered how a relationship needs to be improved? Do you ever worry about your guy being scared away? You don't know how to communicate your love to your guy without freaking him out? Though some men may find it very pleasant to be dramatically loved, most men do not like excessively affectionate women. You need to be able to find a balance that's healthy. Follow these 3 tips to do this:

1 Keep the degree of intimacy under control.

In a relationship, telling your guy that you love him in small ways does a whole lot of good. They are good ways to express great love by offering the occasional massage or cooking something for him. Even, rubbing his arm or hand softly will do wonders. He'll begin to feel smothered if you overwhelm your man with too much affection. Many men don't care for an excessive amount of love, so don't go overboard. Keep affection, especially in front of others, at a low level. In public displays of affection, let him lead.

2 In quiet ways, show him love

Actions speak louder than words, so show him that you love him by using action. These acts are going to show him you care. Never be the first one to tell a man "I love you." Some women realize that this scares men away, but they nevertheless do it. Take your time and, first, let him say it.

3 Let the man take care of you.

In order to make fun memories and develop positive feelings for each other, be sure to continue doing things like going out together. Let him set the pace by doing this and determine how fast the relationship will develop. It will scare him when you take too much influence. He'll feel pressed, and he'll run.

You'll be able to develop a working partnership if you follow these three tips without scaring your special guy away. Make sure that you let him take charge, quietly show him respect, and keep your affection for him in check.

Imagine what if you could make people adore you, pursue you, enjoy you, and devote themselves to you?

We also build lifelong friendships with some of our colleagues as we spend eight hours plus per day at work. We find our perfect partner in certain circumstances at work or across the work network. Even if some of our colleagues, for a wide range of reasons, will never be your friends. Nevertheless, you should always aspire to form at least a decent working relationship with all personalities in a professional setting.

While we sometimes meet individuals with characteristics that we despise, we need to ensure that we establish the right level of individual skills to cultivate good working relationships. If you are part of a team and focus on your appraisals and overall career performance, this is extremely clear. To prevent conflict in your workplace, you should do whatever you can, as it risks undermining your reputation in the business. When you are seen as a good team player and easy to get along with, you can advance well in a organization. You should not become a doormat, however, taking all of this into account. Stand up for your values and opinions always, so that you retain a degree of respect. You need to do this, though, while not infringing on the beliefs of other people and preventing confrontation.

You should: To help you develop outstanding working relationships:

-- Always aim at work to be friendly, respectful and helpful.

-- Please partner with friends on any projects you are involved with.

-- Strive to achieve a role as a superior team worker.

-- Don't be a gentle touch. In order not to lose respect in the department, you need to stand by your convictions.

-- Be a player for the squad. When you have free time to offer your support, be mindful.

-- Never ignore the views of colleagues; be diplomatic and don't argue.

-- Reflect on positive points from colleagues, although they might not be apparent.

-- Do not talk to peers, since this can be a source of dispute.

-- Do not share details about yourself that might lead to rumors about you by others.

-- When they have done well as they respect this, pay compliments to peers and you go up in their confidence.

-- Tell others, without exaggeration, about your achievements. This will build your respect for professionals.

-- If you have a catastrophe, be calm and communicate clearly; stop becoming a drama queen.

-- Plan well for meetings in order to make a constructive contribution.

-- Encourage others to have their say in meetings and respect their opinions.

By the actions you take and the attitudes you demonstrate with colleagues at work, you can damage your career and work relationships. No matter your schooling, your experience, your attitude, or your title, you can never achieve your work mission if you can't play well with others. And, at work, what is your main desire? To accomplish your goal at work.

The foundation of success and happiness with your job and your career is successful interpersonal working relationships. How important are work relationships that are efficient? They form the basis for promotional opportunities, salary rises, achievement of goals, and satisfaction with the work.

Job satisfaction metrics were analyzed by the Gallup organization. They found that one of the twelve primary questions asked of employees that predicted job satisfaction was whether you have a best friend at work. Job satisfaction deteriorates without a friend at work.

What happens when you're not playing with others well?

A manager who served in an organization of several hundred individuals quickly gained a reputation for not playing along with others. In order to find fault, put blame and make other workers look bad, he gathered data and used the data. He enjoyed finding problems and trends of problems, but he never offered solutions.

For a bigger title and more income, he bugged his boss weekly so that he could tell the other workers what to do. Not a single employee recommended that the company take steps to persuade him to stay when he revealed that he was job searching.

All the way along, he had burned his bridges. And when an employer who is checking credentials comes their way, no one would have a positive word to say about him.

The Top 7 ways of playing well at work with others

The top seven ways you can play well with others at work are these. They form the framework for the establishment of successful interpersonal working relationships. In order to create a healthy, inspiring, motivational work environment for people, these are the actions you want to take:

1. Bring to the conference table Suggested alternatives to problems

Some workers spend an excessive amount of time finding issues. Only honestly? The simple part is that. The task that will gain respect and appreciation from your peers and superiors is thoughtful solutions.

Your ability to defend your solution before the team agrees on a stronger or strengthened strategy is also a bonus. Your devotion to implementing the solution eventually selected problems in the development of proposals, too.

2. Don't Play the Blame Game Ever

You alienate colleagues, superiors, and monitoring employees. Yes, you may need to recognize who has been involved in an question. You could also pose the suggested question of Dr. W. Edwards Deming: what caused the employee to struggle with the job scheme? The scheme is the cause of most issues.

3. Matters of the verbal and nonverbal contact

When you talk to another worker, use sarcasm, or sound gross, the other worker hears you. All radar machines which constantly scope out the environment are humans. The message comes out loudly and clearly when you speak to another employee with a lack of respect.

A high-level manager once asked this question of a consultant in one company, I know you don't think I can scream at my staff. But they make me so angry sometimes. When is it ever necessary for me to scream at the staff?

The reply? Never, of course, if respect for people, as it should be, is a hallmark of your company, as it is in massively successful businesses.

4. Never Blind a Coworker, Manager, or Personal Reporting Person

You have blindsided the coworker if the first time a coworker learns about a problem is in a staff meeting or from an email sent to their boss. Often resolve concerns first, with the persons specifically involved who own the work system.

You will never create productive work alliances, also known as ambushing your coworkers, unless your coworkers trust you. And you can never attain the most significant objectives for your job and career without alliances. You can't do this on your own, so treat your colleagues as you want them to treat you.

5. Maintain Your Obligations

Work is interconnected in an organisation. You control the work of other workers if you fail to meet deadlines and obligations. Always maintain promises, and make sure that all impacted workers know what happened, if you can't. Provide a new due date and make every effort possible to respect the new deadline.

It is not okay for a company to allow deadlines to slip by only quietly. Your coworkers will think less of you and disrespect your acts, even though they refuse to confront you. And, no, don't even imagine that they didn't realize for a second that the deadline had passed. If you also accept the chance that they did not care, you disrespect them.

6. Share credit for accomplishments, opinions, and contributions

With no support from others, how often do you reach an objective or complete a project? If you are a manager, how many of the brilliant ideas you support have employee members contributed to?

To thank, reward, recognize and specify the efforts of the individuals who help you excel, take the time and invest the energy. It is a no-fail approach to developing working relationships that are successful. Credit for share; divert blame and loss.

7. Help other workers discover their grandeur

Every employee has skills, abilities, and experience in your company. If you can help fellow staff unlock their best talents, you can support the business tremendously. The creation of individual workers benefits the whole.

Compliment, compliment, and recognize their achievements. To help build a healthy, inspiring atmosphere for workers, you don't have to be a boss. Employees find and contribute their grandeur in this setting in achieving the achievement of the mission and objectives of the company. They're always going to remember you were part of getting it out of them. Those relationships of interpersonal work are cherished.

About the bottom line

If you practice these seven acts on a regular basis, you can play well with others and develop productive interpersonal working relationships. As a colleague, colleagues would trust you. Bosses will think you're competing for them on the correct team.

You will achieve your job goals, and you will also experience satisfaction, gratitude, and personal encouragement. And how can there be any better job than that?

Establish trust with colleagues

Build faith by secrecy and not gossiping. Maintain your appointments and do well with your job. This shows that you can be relied on by others. On your promises, follow through. If you realize that a commitment cannot be kept, apologize and offer to address the matter in another way.

Instead of casting blame on someone or something else, take responsibility for your errors. Integrity is key to faith. Share with coworkers resources and knowledge. You will return materials you borrow promptly.

Operate with your colleagues

Collaborate in a community project for colleagues. Exchange thoughts and be prepared to change the way you normally perform a job. Owe credit for their contributions to others. Provide constructive criticism of your work and seek reviews on it.

Do your share of this job. Volunteering to take on tough tasks. Incorporate fun games and icebreakers into team projects so that participants are better able to know each other. Be an encourager by celebrating others' achievements and encouraging them to do more.

Communicate well by listening clearly and speaking

Develop your communication skills by listening and communicating clearly to others attentively. Echo the sentence in your own terms if you are not sure that you understand the other person, and ask if you understand it correctly. Let others know that their views are respected by you. During talks, maintain eye contact.

Keep your feelings under control, and if anything upsets you, don't use berating expressions. Provide consumers, service providers and other professionals with your calling card so that they can reach you.

Be considerate of others

Demonstrate respect for others. Be knowledgeable in other employees' viewpoints, and be able to discuss points of view that are different from your own. In a courteous way, share your own viewpoints. Avoid sharing long personal stories and sending unrelated job emails.

Limit personal phone calls and distractions, such as radios, if you work in a shared office room. Maintain an attitude of professional and courteous.

Establish trust with colleagues

Build faith by secrecy and not gossiping. Maintain your appointments and do well with your job. This shows that you can be relied on by others. On your promises, follow through. If you realize that a commitment cannot be kept, apologize and offer to address the matter in another way.

Operate with your colleagues

Collaborate in a community project for colleagues. Exchange thoughts and be prepared to change the way you normally perform a job. Owe credit for their contributions to others. Provide constructive criticism of your work and seek reviews on it.

Chapter 9

TEST NEW IDEAS, BOTH IN BUSINESS AND IN INTERPERSONAL RELATIONSHIPS

Change" does not mean zeroing ourselves and starting from scratch. Not only is it wrong, but it's also not possible, our correct thoughts and ways of doing do and will continue to be part of our lives. Even if we do not want them, the changes will still take place, and it is for this reason that we must be able to transform a simple and normal change into real improvement. The only way forward is to test new ideas and believe in them, change that part of yourself that slows down the process of growth and improvement, those patterns of thought or behavior that in different situations still create always identical results. One way to start this process is to take time to study and meditate on your mistakes and learn from them never to repeat them.

Today many of them are born in the world and many of them die, but in this case, as in many other similar situations, failure is experience, knowledge of your sector and opportunities to create new successful initiatives and thus test new ideas. The choice to test new ideas, both in business and in interpersonal relationships, is fundamental to guarantee a progressive positive trend of life and the experiences connected to them, either personal or working.

How to Test Your New Business Ideas?

You've got a brilliant idea and you're prepared to indulge yourself into entrepreneurship. But, are you sure your idea is viable? Before investing in a new business, you need to test your idea's true potential.

Some of the most successful and greatest entrepreneurs and inventors have admitted to failing at some point in their illustrious careers. However, failure is a normal part of business; however, the majority of us are not equipped to "fail efficiently."

He makes his point by using the skiing analogy for teaching entrepreneurs to take deliberate diversions when they are on the road to success. This helps in avoiding catastrophic failures that can lead to personal and financial ruin. Christensen says that during skiing, one does not take his or her skis and point them directly down the mountain because this will result in a severe disaster.

This business approach is poles apart from that taught in business schools. Christensen goes on to say that in business one is taught to conduct performance analysis and set a big goal and directly charge towards it. He says that this approach is the reason for only one in 10 business ventures succeeding.

Instead of bulldozing your way towards a specific goal, slow down and alter your course. This process helps achieve success, and if there is a failure, the business fails "efficiently".

Here are some ways you can test your business idea with target customers:

Have a focus group: A focus group includes a select number of customers who use and provide input on your products. Before you go all in, focus groups, polls, and interviews demonstrate what customers think.

Ask social media groups: Your target market is put at your fingertips by the internet. Find groups online that might be interested in your business. Find out their general impressions and you can do something differently if they think you should.

Set up a page for crowdfunding: Websites for crowdfunding give more than just investors. You may also receive useful reactions from like-minded citizens, insights, and suggestions. Bonus: you could meet someone who wants your idea to be invested in.

Testing the concept on a small group reveals whether customers care about your deals. There's a fair chance your idea would be a hit with a wider audience if the small market tests are successful.

Here are 8 tips to test your new business ideas.

1. Ask the right questions

For your business venture, unclear ideas and partial plans would likely trigger a rough start. You must ask yourself the correct questions to get the answers you need.

Next, take every element of your start-up into account. The questions you ask should help you dig deeper into the process of your thinking and create a strategy. Resolving problems, in the beginning, will help you succeed.

Before you start a company, these questions are examples of what you should think about:

- Why do I want a company to be started?
- What problem am I solving?
- Who is my main customer?
- What tools do I have?
- What are my objectives?

In a journal, you should write down your replies to solidify your feelings. You can start the next steps in testing your business concept as soon as you answer general questions.

2. Know the rivals

You don't want to get too wrapped up with what you do with your rivals. But, knowing their methods is a good thing. Analyze businesses similar to yours before launching your start-up.

You can see what has succeeded in the past by looking at other firms. From others that have already attempted similar concepts, a wise business owner discovers. Because of a failed strategy, you gain useful knowledge without suffering any losses.

It will also help you define what makes your idea stand out by evaluating the competition. You need to show customers how special your company is in order to get a strong customer base. This could be anything from disrupting the market with a new product to delivering an experience that is exclusive.

3. Assess the capital

We have all heard the saying, "It takes money to make money." For a reason, the expression has become a cliche-it is accurate in most instances. To get your start-up off the ground, you will need business capital.

It is likely that start-up funding comes from many sources. Many entrepreneurs finance the expense of starting a new business with personal assets, such as a credit card or a savings account. Others rely on the support of family and friends. For small businesses, banks and private lenders also sell loan services.

Chances are to finance your company; you will need a mix of capital solutions.

The road to securing startup funds could be difficult because you have not yet established yourself as a profitable business. To convince others that your idea is viable, create a small business plan that maps out how you will spend the money and how much you expect to earn.

4. Assess the market

One of the best sources to test your business idea is your target market. Define the dream client and concentrate on who is going to be involved in your offerings. Then do a small group's business research.

5. Care about profitability first

The first advice is to think about profitability first while evaluating your new business ideas. Christensen advises that by concentrating on profitability, new projects begin. He goes on to say that even if there is a small diversion from the overall goal, think of the fastest ways to profitability.

While deciding a pre-fixed amount of resources that you are willing to risk as part of the business venture, whether it's a new business idea or business, Devoting 65% of the capital towards the profitability goal, 25% to resources such as staff, and 10% to scale.

6. Ensure that Failure is Efficient

A new business idea as a failure if profits are not earned within a pre-determined time frame. However, he calls this failure an efficient failure. The time frame for success will differ from business to business depending on how much investment you're ready to make in your venture. Some entrepreneurs will spend years staring at losses before quitting. Efficient failure means not having to spend tons of money and years of hard work if profit is not achieved in the first three months.

7. Focus on Your Goals

After earning profits, the business venture moves towards, which involves the allocation of 65% of resources to staff, structures, and procedures, 25% to scale (through franchising or expansion), and 10% to profitability. This process should continue utilising this resource allocation model that rotates through resources, scale, and profitability, throughout the tenure of the business.

8. Slow Down

You have to admits that organisations that follow the zig-zag principle will take a longer duration of time to achieve their goals. He goes on to say that that by setting clear-cut goals when it comes to people, time, and capital in the business venture, ventures can be more stable and the decrease in speed may give rise to pleasant surprises.

New business ideas involve a considerable amount of risk. With the right approach and the right planning, budding entrepreneurs can taste sweet success within a short period.

Embracing New Business Ideas For Business Growth

For your business to succeed there is a need to come up with sound business management practices especially when it comes to implementing new business ideas. Many business owners have been known to squash on new business ideas even before they have been assessed. They claim their argument on the fact that the ideas have been tried elsewhere and failed.

Since the company may be having other priories, managers take this as an excuse to ignore or put on hold the new business ideas just because they do not embrace them. Good business management calls for putting in place effective and proper evaluation of innovative ideas.

For there to be business growth, managers need to have structures that best help in evaluating and trying new ideas with minimum expense. These ideas have to be examined swiftly to find out if they are worth the try. As a business manager, you need to know the importance of logic management so that no good idea goes to waste and decisive action is taken when necessary.

Creative business management takes into account the risks involved in implementing new ideas and that with proper techniques these ideas can produce positive results. As much as new business innovations are not welcomed or encouraged, as a business owner should learn how to appreciate them.

It may sound like you are playing it safe when you do not leap into a new business idea, but the drawback is seeing the same idea you ignored working out when implemented by your competitor. Rather than stamping on new ideas, put in place systems that would test, implement and even reward individuals that come up with these ideas

Introduction To Building Interpersonal Relationships

Interpersonal relationship refers to a strong association among individuals working together in the same organization. colleagues working together ought to share a special bond for them to deliver their level best. For a healthy interpersonal relationship and ultimately a productive environment at work, individuals need to be frank with each other.

The interpersonal relationships that you develop at work are a vital part of the overall workplace puzzle, with managers and colleagues, or any of your suppliers, and can directly influence your work success and career development.

In this book, you will learn:

- Tips for managing interpersonal relationships
- Different managerial/leadership styles, and how to succeed with each of them

- How to recognize various types of challenging colleagues, and how to interact with them

Why Are Interpersonal Relationships Important?

Interpersonal relationships that you form at work serve a critical role in both your work success and career progress. Positive interpersonal relationships will allow effective communication and understanding among colleagues.

One of the most important relationships you will create when you begin your career is linked to your "boss," and with each new role you take in the future. Make sure that the direction of your management team is supported by what you do and how you work. Know, before you learn how to become a good assistant, you can not become a good leader. Show your managers/colleagues that you are a "team player."

Here are a few methods that you can use to help make your manager (and colleagues) aware that you are dependable and confident in your abilities:

- Show respect.
- Give your best.
- Be honest.
- Keep lines of communication open.
- Maintain boundaries.
- Be positive.
- Manage your emotions.

- Be open to feedback.

Ways To Build Strong, Positive Relationships At Work

It goes without saying that the better our relationships at work, the happier, more engaged and productive we will be. Instead of concentrating our energies on solving the issues that come with negative relationships, we should positively channel our energy to enable us to be more innovative and to concentrate on opportunities free of charge.

Here are seven ways to help create good and productive organizational relationships:

1. Communication that is transparent and truthful

All good relationships depend on communication that is truthful and open. If we're face to face, sending messages or emails, we connect in several ways and it's really important to understand how we interact.

Take time to consider what outcome you want from your communication and use clear and precise language to ensure there is no misunderstanding. The better and more effectively we communicate with those we work with, the more positive and successful the relationship will be.

2. Show appreciation

Genuinely show your appreciation when others help you, whether it is a colleague who has helped you on a difficult project or the junior who has made you a cup of coffee. Everyone enjoys gratitude and needs to feel as though they are making a contribution worth making. A little genuine praise goes a long way to developing good working relationships.

3. Present listening

Reflect on taking the time to listen to your colleagues and customers and see if, in exchange, people will respond to you positively. Active listening is a skill worth actively cultivating, as you will discover that it will help you gain confidence from people quickly.

4. Be constructive

People want happy people to be around. Positivity is infectious and individuals are attracted to people who exhibit positivity. It generates momentum and will improve your relationships with your peers and customers alike.

5. Developing the abilities of your people

When it comes to your unique talents, think about what your strengths and weaknesses are. Be honest and take into account which areas you can gain from working on. Make time to chat face-to-face with colleagues every day, even if it's just five minutes. Continue to develop relationships and demonstrate your concern.

6. Be clear about your needs

Understand what you need from your colleagues and also think about what they need from you. It sounds like common sense but it is worth taking time to consider. Communicating these needs can simplify and strengthen relationships and eliminate misunderstandings. It can also help you progress up the career path if you are clear about your intentions and aspirations.

7. Respect

Respecting the people, you work with ensures that their thoughts and ideas are respected by you. This will allow for productive and innovative working relationships that both parties will benefit from. This will also encourage you to welcome different views from peers and to hear what they have to say.

You need to establish constructive and healthy relationships with your colleagues, customers and other stakeholders in your organization for a successful career.

Think about your working relationships and how you can build and maintain stronger relationships that will help you to feel more engaged, open doors to new ideas, decision making power, opportunities and promotion. After all, the more you put into building positive relationships, the more you will get back.

Why Interpersonal Relationship At The Workplace?

Why do colleagues need to be cordial to each other?

Let us go through the importance of interpersonal relationship at the workplace.

An individual spends around eight to nine hours in his organization and it is practically not possible for him to work all alone. Human beings are not machines who can work at a stretch. We need people with whom we can speak and express our feelings. Imagine working in an agency where there are no friends around!!!!!!!!!! We are social people and we need friends around.

An individual working in isolation is more prone to stress and anxiety. They hardly enjoy their work and attend office just for the sake of it. Individuals working alone find their job monotonous. It is essential to have trustworthy colleagues around with whom one can share all his secrets without the fear of them getting leaked. We must have friends at the workplace who can give us honest feedback.

- A single brain alone can't make all decisions alone. We need people to discuss various issues, evaluate the pros and cons and reach solutions benefiting not only colleagues but also the organization on the whole. The entrepreneur can brainstorm together and reach to better ideas and strategies. Strategies must be discussed on an open platform where every individual has the liberty to express his/her views. colleagues must be called for meetings at least once in a week to promote open communication. Interaction regularly is important for a healthy relationship.
- Interpersonal relationship has a direct effect on the organization culture. Misunderstandings and confusions lead to negativity at the workplace. Conflicts lead you nowhere and in turn spoil the work environment.
- We need people around who can appreciate our hard work and motivate us from time to time. It is important to have some trustworthy workplace colleagues who not only appreciate us when we do a good job, but also tell us our mistakes. In getting the best from others, a pat on the back goes a long way. One wants to have

individuals who are more like mentors than mere peers in the workplace.

- It is still worth getting people around who care about us. In times of crisis, we need colleagues to fall back on themselves. If you do not talk to anyone at the workplace, no one would come to your help when you need them.
- An individual needs to get along with colleagues to complete assignments within the stipulated time frame. An Individual working all alone is overburdened and never finishes tasks within deadlines. Support of fellow workers is important. You just can't do everything on your own. Roles and responsibilities must be delegated as per specialization, educational qualification and interests of colleagues. An individual needs help of his colleagues to complete assignments on time and for better results.

Building Great Work Relationships

Making Work Enjoyable and Productive

How good are the relationships that you have with your colleagues?

People who have a best friend at work are seven times more likely to be interested in their careers, according to an organization. And it doesn't have to be a best friend: it's more likely that people who have simply had a good friend at work are satisfied.

We're looking at how you can create strong, meaningful relationships at work in this book. We'll see why getting good working relationships is vital, and we'll look at how to improve your relationships with people that you don't get on with naturally.

Why have relationships that are good?

Naturally, human beings are social creatures-we want friendship and positive interactions, just as food and water do. So, it makes sense that the better our relationships are at work, the happier and more productive we're going to be.

Good working relationships give us several other benefits: our work is more enjoyable when we have good relationships with those around us. Also, people are more likely to go along with changes that we want to implement, and we're more innovative and creative.

What's more, good relationships give us freedom: instead of spending time and energy overcoming the problems associated with negative relationships, we can, instead, focus on opportunities.

Good relationships are also often necessary if we hope to develop our careers. After all, if you're not trusted by your manager, it's unlikely that when a new job opens up, he or she will consider you. Overall, we all want to collaborate with individuals with whom we're on good terms.

In our professional circle, we also require good working relations with others. For our performance, colleagues and key stakeholders are all important. So, building and maintaining good relations with these people is important.

Defining a strong relation

Nice, healthy working relationships are made up of many characteristics:

Trust-This is the basis of any good link. You form a powerful bond when you trust your team and colleagues, which helps you to work and communicate more effectively. You can be open and honest about your thoughts and decisions if you trust the people you work with and you do not have to waste time and energy "watching your back."

Mutual Respect-You value their feedback and ideas when you respect the people you work with and they value yours. You will create ideas based on your mutual experience, wisdom and imagination by working together.

Mindfulness-This implies taking responsibility for your acts and words. Those who are mindful are careful and attend to what they say, and they don't let their own negative emotions impact the people around them.

Welcoming Diversity - People with good relationships not only accept diverse people and opinions, but they welcome them. For example, you take the time to hear what they have to say and consider their input into your decision-making power when your friends and colleagues give different viewpoints than yours.

Open Communication-We chat all day long, whether we send emails and IMs, or face to face meetings. The more you connect with people around you and more efficiently, the richer your relationships will be. On open honest communication, all good relationships rely.

Difficult Relationships

Occasionally, you'll have to deal with anyone you don't like or anyone you really can't communicate with. But you must maintain a professional relationship with him for the sake of your job.

When this occurs, make an attempt to get to know the person. She probably knows full well that the two of you are not on the best terms, so make the first move by involving him in a sincere conversation or inviting him out for lunch to strengthen the relationship.

While you're talking, try not to be too guarded. Ask him about his background, interests and past successes. Instead of putting energy into your differences, focus on finding things that you have in common.

Just note, not all relationships are going to be perfect, but you should make sure they are workable, at least!

This book gives you the abilities you need for a good and happy career, and this is only one of the many resources and tools you can find here.

ex. "I would appreciate if you could leave a review on…"

Chapter 10

TIPS AND TRICKS TO TAKING CONTROL OF YOUR LIFE

Courage for change - Overcome the limits of your mind

It takes courage to take the first step! Courage is not the absence of fear, but the ability not to be stopped by it and therefore want to face it, aware of knowing how to do it. Remember that the more you focus on fear, the more you will empower it, and the less decision-making power you will have! It takes courage to take the first steps to transform your habits and your ways of acting and "thinking wrong" rooted in time, but once you have made the way to achieve excellent results it is wide open, and your business will also have a real chance to take off.

You will realize that the change has occurred only when the new situation that has been created or the new behavior that you have, no longer needs efforts to remain so, but has become pleasant and automatic. So, you started to transform your habits and broadened your range of action in your life and as a reflection in your business. All this do it now because now is the time to act, don't wait for tomorrow, because tomorrow is the future and it will find you unprepared. Act now and don't procrastinate because now is the best time to act and improve your business cards.

Turning the weakness into strength

Pleasure and pain are two great engines that push you to action, so use them to find the motivation that you have perhaps lacked so far to make that decision.

For the business it is the first step that affects you enormously for what it brings, fears, questions, who knows and your flaws, but if you think about how to exploit those weak points by changing them into strengths, if think about how to transform habits into novelties, if you think about how to have a personal decision-making power, if you focus on what you want and act accordingly, all this will allow you to forge the right character to make your business take off.

How to turn shortcomings into strengths

Do not restrict the goods of your organization to activities that are just within your comfort zone. You can find you have opened up a whole new market and revenue stream if you stretch yourself a little.

This one sounds a little wild, you might know, but keep reading. I'm not saying that anyone is going out and making more vulnerabilities. No, that's not the way anyone in an organization is going to make a living wage. Nor can you win many customers by saying that's what you're doing.

Ask consumers about what their needs are.

Instead of only presenting consumers with the same old deals, ask them what they want or need. It might be somewhat close to what you offer, but it's just enough different to give you a learning opportunity while you get paid for it. Ultimately, you'll have something new to show the next customer. This is how most of my offerings in consulting practice have emerged.

How you can turn weaknesses in company into strengths

Face it, in all, you can't be healthy. Here's how to compensate for the talents you lack.

You will be fantastic at everything you need in a perfect world to have a successful business and a successful life. Then again, you will have beautiful hair, abs of steel, and a winning lottery ticket in your pocket in the perfect world, too.

We all have to face the fact here in this imperfect world that we're decent at some things, only passable at others, and outright bad at others that are critical. This can be frustrating if you are an entrepreneur, because you want to be amazing at it. Worse, since you're the only one who can make your business a success, you might believe you have to be good at everything. Okay, guess what? In all, you're not fine, and neither is anyone else.

What would you do, then? Find ways to turn the greatest weaknesses into strengths.

This is how:

1. Recognize your shortcomings and embrace them.

If you are busy denying that weakness exists, you can't turn a weakness into a power. So the first step is to admit that you have limitations and assess what they are.

Only take me. I'm not good at questioning myself. Or rather, I'm really good at conflict avoidance. Often this was beneficial for me, but other times it created needless trouble. So many times, due to my inability to have an uncomfortable experience, I've let a bad situation last for too long. I'm not proud of this, but it's helpful to confess that to myself. It means that when making choices on what to do, I should take this tendency into account.

2. Have someone you trust with guidance.

I found about a year ago that two individuals I trusted were actively trying to undermine me. I felt hurt and betrayed, and I followed my long-standing — and conflict-avoiding — practice of keeping the dispute under wraps while I addressed the matter with them privately.

But I have asked for the advice of a very wise friend who is much less afraid of unpleasantness than I am. She strongly urged me to put the matter into the open for debate. I gave it some thought and then followed her advice, recognizing that my inability to start a confrontation could be working against me.

It was the decision that was correct. Bringing the dispute into the open put an end to the deals in the backroom and helped me take control of the situation. I wish I could have seen for myself the need. But it worked just as well to realize that I needed advice and get it from someone smarter than me.

3. Be pretty prepared.

Often, overcompensating with outstanding planning is the best defence against weakness. I have a very bad sense of direction, for instance, and I tend to get lost, even though it would be a simple matter for someone else to find my way. For someone who likes to fly as much as I do, it is an unavoidable weakness. So, with a GPS in my car, another one on my computer, and the third one on my mobile, where I also download local maps for offline use, I'm using technology to save myself. I hold a detailed paper map in some locations, as well.

In other contexts, similar techniques can apply. About signing a deal with conditions that are unknown? Learn up in advance. Does a client or investor need to pitch for the first time? Learn everything you can about the person you're pitching and then practice your pitch on your colleagues or friends a few times.

4. Hire the talents you lack.

You're better off hiring someone who can fill in the abilities you lack, either as a contractor or full time, instead of doing something that you're not good at. In addition to compensating for your weakness, this will help you build up a valuable ability you need — finding and then trusting workers you can trust. There is no greater measure of confidence than offering others a job that you don't completely understand and then moving out of the way. And there's no better way to inspire the people working for you.

5. Get good enough, get good enough.

Although you can never be great at all assignments, some are valuable enough that it is worth the extra effort to learn more, practice, and attain basic competence. A very smart entrepreneur I once met, even though he had no technological skills, he headed up an internet business. He needed to understand more about what they did, even though he trusted his staff, to be able to tell when they could reach deadlines and when they just couldn't, what was really possible and what wasn't.

That's an insightful solution. There are many things that we should all be able to do on our own, to some extent at least. If you're going to recruit and manage individuals doing those jobs, that's particularly true.

6. Look for ways of helping those with the same problem.

As they say, the mother of creativity is aggravation. If not having an ability you need is an issue for you, you can be sure that it is also an issue for others. Many successful launches come about because the creator wanted him or herself for that product or service. So think of ways you can support yourself and others to make up for your weakness. Your weakness could wind up leading to a new successful venture for you.

Mental Attitude

It's all here! Your mental attitude unequivocally determines the quality of your life and your business. Any right result you want to achieve can only be achieved if you decide to grab it and you are convinced that you can do it. To take control of your life, test new ideas, transform your habits and have great decision-making power, you must be convinced that you have the potential to do it, you have the desire to complete this path and you have the will to pursue it and reach it.

How to transform the mental attitude from negative to positive

Attitude begins with a thought

It has been estimated that every 24 hours, the average person has about 60,000 individual thoughts. 95% of these thoughts are the same as they were the day before, and 80% of these recurring thoughts are negative / pessimistic in nature. In addition, many of these pessimistic thoughts are unconscious and habitual, which means that individuals have almost no knowledge of the influence these thoughts have on their lives.

What is perhaps more troubling is that 95% of the thoughts that people have form the basis of the feelings that they feel during the day. This is important because our feelings form the basis of our attitude, and in all aspects of life, our attitude is what forms our happiness and success.

What are reflections?

Thoughts are biochemical impulses that carry magnetic properties for energy, intellect, and knowledge. Inside each cell, these magnetic properties emerge and are affected by your peer groups, worldviews, cultural history, media, mythology and social norms as a result. The ideas you have about yourself, about others and your life and circumstances are influenced and colored by all these elements of life. Over time, these ideas develop into beliefs from views.

Convictions are nothing more than a formula for ideas "locked" into place. There is no uncertainty or desire or hope when you have a conviction about something. Things are the way they are and no alternative view exists. To form a part of the puzzle that forms your mood during the day, you have "locked" a certain collection of thoughts in place.

Let's break this down in a different way: your feelings are the outcome of life. Because of how you have been affected by 'life,' you have the feelings you have. Life entails what is now, what has been in the past, and what is likely to take place in the future. As such, your opinions and behaviors are the product of your peer groups, worldviews, cultural history, pressures from the media, and other social variables. In other words, you have the feelings you have because, in a certain and unique way, you have encountered life. Therefore, because of the influences you have accepted into your life-into your mind-you are as you are today.

You've decided to concentrate on certain things over a lifetime, while avoiding other things. In this country, there are so many different viewpoints and perspectives. You have only decided to concentrate on a handful of them, however. Your friends, parents, teachers, mentors, cultural history have somewhat pushed some of them upon you. Other items, however, that you have decided to concentrate on because of your personal interests and tastes. Therefore, through the decisions you have made over a lifetime, you have developed your present thought patterns and viewpoints.

Thoughts don't turn into attitudes right away. It is a time-consuming process. For example, you will have an initial thought about something. In your brain, this idea activates different cells. The more you use this "think" by repetition, the more basic cells you use, and the stronger the connection between those cells becomes. Likewise, the more emotional energy that goes into a thought, the stronger the brain's neural highway is. As such, next time around, the simpler it is to have that particular "think". The idea gradually becomes a habit and is projected as a mindset into the real world, which is nothing more than a series of emotions, beliefs, views, and values.

A thinking is never an isolated phenomenon. By connecting current situations to memories, the brain still seeks to make sense of the universe. This link between the past and the present shapes the brain's connections that help you make the world better. Of course, you will discover something fresh and different, but your brain will always try to find some relevance, and will thus find a way to connect the new to the old.

How your brain ties old memories to new experiences will dictate how you make sense of the world. And how you make sense of the world shapes how you think of your world, which forms the basis of what you believe in your world, manifesting the mindset you are projecting into the world.

Thoughts are as complicated as they are simple. Due to their existence, they are easy. It's easy to have a thought, but it's not easy to understand how that thought came to be, or what the implications in the future would be of having that thought. As such, the thoughts are constructs that are very complex because they are affected by several different variables.

Remember one of your thoughts for a moment, and ask yourself:

- Why did I have this particular thought?
- Why now? Why is that so? Why not a particular thing?
- How did this thought come about?

- Where did this idea come from?
- What inspired that idea in my life?
- How many distinct variables affected it?
- How far back in my childhood may this thought be linked to its origins?
- How have other facets of my psyche affected this thought?

There are several components of the psyche that come to form the MasterMind Matrix. As such, your thoughts are affected not only by external stimuli, but also by the response of pain and pleasure, your beliefs, self-concept, meta-programs, psychological laws, mental concentration, decisions, power-making decisions, behavior, physiology, language, etc. Similarly, your emotions are affected by all these "pieces" of your conduct and psyche. In other words, not only are these aspects of your psyche affecting your thoughts, but these "parts" still affect and form your thoughts. And all listed here, TOGETHER, forms your attitude-for better or worse.

The essentials of an attitude

In many ways, your attitude is nothing more than a set of your ideals, beliefs and the views you have on a particular subject. Your emotions form these parts of your psyche, and your thoughts are formed by the world in which you live, by your experiences, and as a result of the things you have chosen over a lifetime to reflect on.

In your life, whatever you give your attention to becomes a priority. Therefore, whatever you want to concentrate on has importance for you, and as a result, these factors will influence how you think, what you believe, what you respect, and, in turn, the mindset you are going to project into the world.

Two fundamental rules are at stake here.

The Law of Concentration is the first of these rules, and the Law of Being is the second of these laws.

1. Concentration Law: The Concentration Law states that in your life, what you think, emotionalize, and imagine continues to evolve.

2. The Law of Becoming: The Law of Becoming states that after your dominant thought patterns, you transform yourself. In other words, following the emotions you have decided to focus on most frequently throughout the day, you draw into your life your weaknesses, talents, shortcomings, and abilities.

These two Universal Laws suggest that the whole of your life and the mindset that you project into the world depends much of the time on what you want to concentrate on. Therefore, if your attitude is bad and you want to make a change, then you have to choose to reflect on other things that can help you change your feelings, thus enhancing your attitude.

Your stance is also related to the examples you have gathered over a lifetime.

A collection of memories is formed from any experience you have- whether good or bad, painful or pleasurable. These recollections build references that you use to make sense of the world in which you live. These references are only encounters that have come about in your life as a consequence of pain and pleasure. For example, in the past, you may have encountered a negative circumstance that gave you unpleasant memories. Or in the past, you might have encountered a good scenario that gave you pleasurable memories. Such situations / experiences today are nothing more than memories. These memories / references, however, have a huge influence on the mindset that you are projecting out into the world.

Naturally, your brain can connect several painful memories / references to shape an opinion on something. As more associated sources are found, these opinions improve over time. And these references come over the long term to shape your views about this particular circumstance or area of your life. And as a result, these values form the basis of the mindset that you are projecting out into the world.

Now, it's important to remember that only opinions are these memories / references. They are all your opinions and perceptions of the scenario. In fact, they may have no actual basis. As such, your attitude can be focused on false references that you have accepted as the reality, and skewed memories. Therefore, your pessimistic attitude is based on a "lie" which you have persuaded yourself to believe. And this affects how you feel, think, and behave for better or worse in particular circumstances. Perhaps worse, it changes your perceptions of yourself, of others and of the world around you. This, thus, causes a "snowball" effect in which a negative mindset develops and gathers momentum over time before your life is ruined.

You could feel some really severe pain one day after years of living with a negative mental attitude that results from the attitude you are constantly projecting into the world. It is this traumatic experience that will also give you the "wake-up" call you need to make those changes for the better. But you don't need to wait, in all honesty, before this moment happens. Today-right now-you should start making positive changes!

Creating a favorable mental outlook

The ability to perceive and reframe your life experiences in a favorable way that is supportive and conducive to the desired outcomes you would like to achieve is a positive mental attitude (PMA). It is the capacity during tough times to foster optimism. In other words, it's a "solution-focused" strategy that searches for solutions to grievances.

It takes time and practice to cultivate a PMA. It's not something that you'll get into the habit of doing instantly. You're going to have to make some changes, start doing things differently, and make some better decisions. However, it will be an effort worth investing, as it will help open the door to very different viewpoints and a world full of new possibilities.

Now, let 's look at some easy things you can do to help improve how you think about your life and situations that can facilitate a PMA.

Enable comparisons of self-to-self

Making similarities is human nature. Some individuals make comparisons with others, while others compare their "best selves." At some occasions, both are beneficial. Self-to-other comparisons, for example, help you gauge where other individuals are, and this helps drive your competitive spirit. It can also, however, make you feel incompetent and unworthy if you struggle to live up to the expectations and results of other people. There are self-to-self comparisons, on the other hand. It's beneficial to make these distinctions because you're competing against your best selves.

All of this is important to actions since a bad mental attitude is often related to associations between others and oneself. In an effort to make ourselves feel better about ourselves, we knowingly or unconsciously equate ourselves to others. Nevertheless, if we are unable to live up to the expectations that other people set, then it's easy to feel somewhat insignificant and incomplete. And it is from this position that a mental attitude that is pessimistic always comes to the surface and expresses itself in excuses and grievances.

Choose instead to make just self-to-self comparisons to prevent this situation. Compare yourself to your best self and leave other people with self-to-other comparisons.

Ask questions that are effective

If you are aware of it consciously or not, you are always asking questions. Some questions are helpful, while others may not be so helpful, which may appear to prolong a bad mental attitude, thus.

The best thing about questions is that they help focus your concentration and attention to particular items. If you concentrate on the negative and on what doesn't work, for example, then you will begin to feel miserable, and that will come out in the mindset you are projecting into the world. However, as you reflect on what works, what you have, and what you can handle, then your mindset changes as well. You do not feel remorse, sadness, or lament about things anymore. Instead, you are focused on the stuff that will make you move more confidently forward.

In exactly this way, questions will help you guide your "focus". Of course, though, you will need to ask yourself the right kinds of questions to help concentrate your mind on the stuff that will help foster a healthy mental attitude. Here are some examples of questions that you can probably ask yourself:

- What's great about it?
- What prospects are there?
- How will I develop from this experience?
- How do I make myself feel wonderful about it?
- How can this be seen in a more constructive light?
- How do I change my strategy?

You concentrate on items that matter the most by taking the time to honestly answer these questions. These "stuff" will help you see the situation in a better light and will place you in a more optimal and optimistic frame-of-mind. And your attitude shifts as your emphasis changes, and you then put yourself in a more favorable position to make the most of any circumstance and opportunity.

Associate with People Inspiring

There is an explanation why you might have a bad mentality. And it also comes down to the business that you retain.

The attitude that you are actively projecting into the world undoubtedly resembles your peers' attitude very closely. So, if their attitude is bad, then your attitude would be poor as well. If they still complain, make excuses, blame and dwell on issues, then you probably do this as well. This is not going to be valid in all situations, of course. However, for the most part, as much as you mimic their attitude, your five closest peers / friends will always reflect your attitude. For this very reason, you must very carefully choose the individuals you want to hang out with.

Think and remind yourself about any of your closest friends and confidants:

- How are these individuals affecting me?
- Do I complain about the same stuff that they are complaining about?
- Do I blame others in the same way that others are blamed?
- Do I make reasons that are similar?
- What did these individuals make me think?
- What did these people tell me?
- What did these individuals emotionalize me for?
- How do these individuals affect my state-of-mind?

- How do they affect the mentality I'm projecting out into the world?

If you take the time to ask yourself these questions frankly, I think you're going to find that your peers have a greater effect on your mindset than you could have expected initially-for better or worse. If it's on the "worse" side, then you might want to rethink with whom you spend the most time. Choose people who encourage you to see your life and situations more favorably and optimally and question you. In itself, that is one of the fastest ways to change a bad mental attitude.

The 4 phases of transition

You can usually go through four different phases before making any changes in your life:

- Acceptance: "I just can't adjust ..."
- Recognition: "I should really adjust ..."

Initially, you embrace the fact that you are powerless to adjust. You are resistant to change at this point and struggle with the idea that things must change regardless of how bad things may be. Yeah, maybe your attitude isn't perfect, but there isn't enough pain to instigate a shift.

The second step is to recognize that change is important and that you need to start doing things that will help you make meaningful changes in your life. This is where the pain sets in, and you know in the long run that the effects of not improving are too expensive and hurtful.

The third step is your decision that a change needs to be made. You do not want to indulge in a bad mental attitude anymore, and you want to be different instead-you want to make a positive difference for the better. And it is really in these "decision" moments that the seeds of progress are planted.

The final phase of this process is the statement that you are no longer your "old" self, but rather a "new" self that has changed for the better. And because you see yourself as this new person, you begin to make numerous choices and decisions that are consistent with this new person's feelings, values, beliefs, and attitudes.

You will usually go through each of these steps as you progress through this attitude change process. This process may take time, but even the most stubborn of behaviors can be transformed with a little consistent effort.

CONCLUSION

It all comes down to the mentality that you project out into the universe when it comes to success in every area of endeavor. You can make bad decisions if your attitude is poor, and you can very well create needless disputes and problems for yourself.

When your mindset comes from an empowering state-of - mind, moreover, this can lead to greater decision-making capacity that will help you overcome challenges and take advantage of the possibilities that life gives you. As such, your mindset lets you take charge of your life and forms the base of what you want in life to do, be, have and accomplish.

The planet is your oyster with a good mental mindset. The universe would just rub dirt in your face without it.

A LETTER FOR YOU

Dear Reader,

I want to thank you from the bottom of my heart for choosing my book. As the author, it would please me to know in what way "***Take Control of your life ...while you drink a coffee***" was helpful to you or simply what positive reflections you made. I won't deny that it is also a personal satisfaction to know that this book has added value and quality to your life. I would appreciate it if you could share your impressions of what you liked with your friends and acquaintances by posting on your favorite Social. I'd really love to hear your story, know how you feel, what progress you've made or what life lesson you consider most relevant in your case.

What you can read in about 10 minutes is actually the result of many hours of work, reflection, memories of my experience and others, research and scientific insights. I never thought it would take so much time and effort to write a book. That's why I would really appreciate it if you could give me your feedback by posting your honest review on Amazon. Any feedback will be of great help to me in improving this book and the writing of the next ones. Leave me your review now by following this link or QRcode

https://www.amazon.com/gp/customer-reviews/write-a-review.html?asin=B08XFK9VP7

You will have my gratitude and that of all those readers who, like you, are looking for a useful and compelling book. Please do so now!

Also, to stay in touch, I invite you to follow me on my blog www.texjerhand.com so you'll be informed about the books I publish and you can also receive a welcome giveaway.

I wholeheartedly wish you the best and a future of great success.

10 Ways of Thinking **is part of a series of books.**

You can deepen or integrate this information by reading other books on the same topic as. You can search for them in **Amazon Kindle** by writing "**10 ways of thinking**" or take a look at some of the titles that may interest you.

***If you've come to read this far, it means that the topic is of interest to you, don't hesitate:* try, order the book now!**

CPSIA information can be obtained
at www.ICGtesting.com
Printed in the USA
BVHW040940110321
602201BV00025B/217

9 781914 360039